THE DESTRUCTION
OF THE KINGDOM

This is VOLUME SIX of
THE BIBLE IN HISTORY
edited by Joseph Rhymer

Edited by Father Robert Tamisier, P.S.S.

*Advisory Editor for the English
Language Edition:* Joseph Rhymer

Editorial Consultants:

Father Edward J. Ciuba

Bishop John J. Dougherty

Rabbi Samuel Sandmel

Dr Samuel L. Terrien

The Destruction of the Kingdom

by HENRI GAUBERT

Translated by Lancelot Sheppard

A Giniger Book
published in association with
HASTINGS HOUSE, PUBLISHERS
NEW YORK

CONTENTS

1

THE PURPOSE OF THIS BOOK

All historical accounts are selective. That should be an obvious thing to say. It would be quite impossible to describe every detail of every aspect of an event, and even then it would be necessary to show how the details were related to each other, how they fitted in with the total pattern. The historian selects the details and connections which interest him or his readers, or he selects one particular pattern from the many patterns which can be found in the events about which he is writing. This process of selection and deliberate patterning is easy to see in such a work as the description of a town. One writer may emphasise the town's industries and skills. Another writer may describe the leisure facilities and the opportunities for people who wish to spend a holiday there. Yet another may concentrate on a new housing development with exciting architectural features. Each writer would claim that what he had written was true and complete, within the subject which he had chosen for his book.

All this should be obvious, but we are easily disturbed if we find the same forces at work in the books of the Bible, and particularly in the historical books. The historical books in the Bible are further complicated by two factors. Firstly, the 'author' of the final form of the book was using material which had already been selected and shaped by many people before it reached him. Such a final author was sometimes writing and editing his book several centuries after the events he was describing. The differing points of view of many people had already left their mark on the information that was available to him. But the second factor is even stronger: the author was not writing a merely descriptive work. His main purpose in writing was not to inform his readers but to change them. It was history brought to bear on the present, contemporary situation, to help the people who had to solve the contemporary problems.

There are two main groups of historical writings in the Old Testament, the Deuteronomic histories and the Priestly histories. They were written about the same events, but for different purposes and situations. The Deuteronomic books are Judges, 1 & 2 Samuel and 1 & 2 Kings. The Priestly books are Joshua and 1 & 2 Chronicles. The Deuteronomic authors are closely connected with the reform carried out by King Josiah in 621 B.C.; they are interested in social justice, Jerusalem as a religious centre guarded and served by the king, and in a strict doctrine of reward and retribution by God. Their main work was written during the earlier part of the exile in Babylon when there was still hope that the nation would be restored under the Davidic rule of the monarchy, despite the disasters which successive kings had brought upon their people. The Priestly authors were writing at the end of the Babylonian exile when the people needed encouragement as they set about rebuilding Jerusalem and restoring the national economy. The main themes here are the invincible power of God which can be seen at work in the history of his chosen people, the importance of the sacrifices offered and controlled by properly authorised

priests, and the absolute authority of the law. The monarchy had failed and had been replaced by the rule of
immutible divine law.

A modern author who attempts to set the Bible in
its historical context is faced with a constant dilemma:
should he continually point out the purposes and beliefs
which have shaped the material he finds in the Bible,
or should he be content with pointing out the main
events which have inflenced the historical writings in
the Bible and leave the rest to the reader? In this work
the second of these possibilities has been the one
selected.

JOSEPH RHYMER

2

ISRAEL AND JUDAH
AT VARIANCE (931–926)

We begin this chapter with serious apprehensions, with the feeling that we are entering on a very disturbed period. We shall witness, in fact, four centuries of tragedy which conclude with the almost complete destruction of the People of God, and the deportation to Babylon of the 'remnant' of Judah. But in the very depths of misfortune there is already the promise of the rebirth of Israel, of an Israel regenerated in the crucible of fearful trials.

In 931 Solomon had just died. This ostentatious king left behind him a disturbing situation: an empty treasury, a country ruined by taxes, religion in a state of decadence, and among the mass of the people a clearly-marked spirit of revolt with some tendency to separatism.

The future was gloomy but not desperate. Rehoboam, Solomon's son and successor, could well have guided the country on a course that would save it from disaster. It remained to be seen if he were capable of performing this providential role.

Rehoboam at the cross roads

The problem facing Rehoboam was a political one certainly, but still more it was a psychological one. The facts were these.

Ever since they had settled in the land of Canaan (in

about 1200 B.C.) and until the accession of David (1010) the Twelve Tribes, traditionally descended from Abraham's grandson, Jacob, were divided into two distinct groups. In the north of Palestine, and spread out, roughly speaking, over the left bank of the Jordan, was the first federation traditionally designated by the name of Israel. In addition, in the southern zone, was another group, also belonging to the Yahwist religion, which was known as Judah; it was made up of the tribe of the same name together with the remains of the tribe of Simeon and various small clans. (See Map, p. 12.)

At this juncture David appeared. He was of the tribe of Judah and a statesman of genius; he quickly saw that to ensure the survival of the Twelve Tribes in Canaan, it was urgently important to organise the political and military unification of all the sons of Jacob. The safety of the People of God depended on it.

The new leader was well aware, we can be sure, of the antipathy shown on all occasions by Israel, the Yahwist group of the north, towards Judah, the Yahwist group of the south. When he had finally achieved the union of Israel and Judah in one kingdom he made every endeavour to rule with the greatest tact and the strictest justice in a situation made delicate by the uncertain temper of the northern tribes.

Logically, David's successors had only to continue this skilful policy and the people would soon forget their old divisions.

Solomon succeeded David in 970. Contrary to expectation, the young king took an opposite course from that of his father. He very soon began a vast building programme. To ensure that he had sufficient masons and labourers to work the various sites he decided to enrol the able-bodied men of the kingdom in forced labour gangs, such as had been used for thousands of years in

Egypt and Mesopotamia. Thus the majority of the peasants were requisitioned to work, under the overseer's lash and rod, in terrible living conditions on the many buildings projected by Solomon.

We have already seen something of the mentality of these descendants of the nomad shepherds who, scarcely two centuries previously, had been established in the Promised Land. Once they had settled most of them became farmers. But they did not lose the spirit of freedom and independence of their ancestors, the nomads of the plains. Then suddenly they were torn from their families and lands to be interned in labour camps often at a great distance from their homes. They were forced to make bricks, haul enormous tree trunks or place in position great blocks of stone. This form of life, with its very high death-rate, was in all respects like that of a convict settlement. The sons of Jacob had already experienced forced labour in Egypt at the time of Rameses II (1301–1234), who also had a passion for building temples and palaces of colossal size. But now the despot who ruled over the followers of Yahweh, was, derisively enough, the Lord's anointed, a sovereign to whom God had entrusted the destiny of his beloved people.

It was understandable, therefore, that the labourers from Judah should mutter against Solomon, their fellow countryman. Even more easily can we understand the hatred of the Israelites from the north condemned to toil under such hardship for the glory of a king from the south. And yet both had to keep silent and continue their toil, for the police service was well organized: any subversive remark was reported and punished.

After Solomon's death Rehoboam, his son, seemed the obvious successor. He was then about forty years old; he had reached maturity. Would he, it was wondered, return to the wise traditions of government of his grandfather David, or would he continue the fateful policy of Solomon?

It was a critical moment for the history of the Chosen People.

Rehoboam proclaimed king of Judah; will he also be proclaimed king of Israel? (1 Kings 12; 2 Chron. 10)
At Jerusalem Rehoboam was proclaimed king by the assembly of the elders. It was understandable that the southern chieftains should readily accept as sovereign a man of their own tribe.

To the northerners the problem was somewhat different. They were not indeed opposed in principle to giving their allegiance to a king from Judah provided that he agreed to abolish forced labour, the source of so much misery and death.

In order to establish the basis of an agreement and to discuss questions of government the men of Israel invited Rehoboam to go to Shechem, a city of the tribe of Ephraim, and one of the most celebrated religious cities of the north, to discuss the questions of government. There, unexpectedly, Rehoboam found himself face to face with Jeroboam, who has previously appeared very briefly in the story of Solomon.

Jeroboam was a man of Israel, from the tribe of Ephraim. Of humble origins, he had been sent to Jerusalem to take charge of a group of his fellow countrymen who were building the great rampart of the Temple promenade. On this occasion Solomon was able to notice the intelligence and energy of this young man, and shortly afterwards put him in charge of the labourers of the *house of Joseph* (the popular name of the federation of Israel).

In the ordinary course of events it looked as if Jeroboam would be quickly promoted to a high post in the organization of the royal building projects. But on the advice of the prophet Ahijah (an Ephraimite again) Jeroboam suddenly changed sides; he soon took the part of his fellow countrymen of Israel, who were being treated so harshly by Solomon. He placed himself at the head of a movement of rebellion. Solomon's police were soon on the scent of the nascent plot. To save his head Jeroboam took to flight and found refuge in Egypt at the court of the pharaoh Sheshonk, the head of a new dynasty which made no secret of its feelings of hostility for the king of Jerusalem.

On the news of Solomon's death Jeroboam hastened to leave his place of exile to return to his home in Ephraim where his fellow-countrymen welcomed him with enthusiasm. It was not long before he was entrusted with a delicate mission; he was required to defend the interests of Israel during the official interview that had been requested of Rehoboam.

Rehoboam's foolish answer (1 Kings 12; 2 Chron. 10)

Negotiations began on a conciliatory tone; the demands made by Israel were by no means excessive: *'Your father gave us a heavy burden to bear; lighten your father's harsh tyranny now, and the weight of the burden he laid on us, and we will serve you.'* This was a reference to the heavy taxes and to the forced labour, whose abolition was demanded by the men of Israel. Rehoboam asked for a delay of three days for reflection before giving an answer.

Consulted by their king the elders of Judah made no secret of the fact that the time had come for concessions. This was very wise. But Rehoboam's immediate entourage, composed of his young companions, were impatient to enjoy the pleasures of absolute power. They urged him to reject with scorn any discussion with his subjects. According to the traditions of the east, they must toil in order to ensure a pleasant life for their rulers. At the end of the three-day period Rehoboam was in a position to give his answers to the elders of Israel. *'My father made you bear a heavy burden,'* he said, *'but I will make it heavier still. My father beat you with whips; I am going to beat you with loaded scourges.'*

He could hardly have been more overbearing or blundering. His ill-considered remarks showed clearly that he intended to continue his father's harsh policy.

Israel refuses to accept the king of Judah's absolutism
(1 Kings 12:16)

At Rehoboam's declaration the representatives of Israel at once uttered a warcry. Repeating an old refrain of the separatist party, which had secretly remained in existence in Ephraim, these men of the north began to sing the song of rebellion:

> *'What share have we in David?*
> *We have no inheritance in the son of Jesse.*
> *To your tents, Israel.'*[1]

And Israel, the biblical account continues, *went off to their tents.* The incident is reported briefly. In point of fact it was a real revolution which broke out at the building sites in the south where several groups from Israel were working; workers left the buildings in course of construction all over the territory; they returned in groups to their native land.

---

[1] *David:* that is, the government of Israel was to remain independent of the government of Judah whose founder was David. *Jesse:* this was David's father, a farmer in the neighbourhood of Bethlehem. *To your tents:* this means that negotiations were over and that all should return home. Note the archaic character of the phrase: at this period Jacob's descendants no longer lived in tents, they had settled on the land and now lived in houses. All the same, in everyday language they retained expressions going back to the far-off days when the Hebrew shepherds wandered on the plains, following their sheep.

Rehoboam, always presumptious, imagined that he could put down the rebellion at once. To recall the rebels to their duty he sent his superintendent of labour, Adoram. The Israelites at once stoned him to death; he was cordially hated by the labourers, for he had always treated them with terrible hashness. When Rehoboam himself arrived he was badly received, and to avoid being put to death himself he was obliged to mount his chariot and flee back to Jerusalem.

And Israel has been separated from the House of David until the present day. David's great work of unification had not even lasted a century.

The tragedy was twofold: it was a political separation and a religious schism, both of which had incalculable consequences.

Israel and Judah: the political separation (1 Kings 12:20–25; 2 Chron. 10:19)

Without delay the Ten Tribes of the north, known under the name of Israel[2] proclaimed their independence and at once named their ruler – Jeroboam. He was the obvious choice for the elders of Ephraim and he was chosen as king.

Between these two States the frontier was established following a line passing a short distance below Bethel (see map, p. 12); this enabled Judah to incorporate within its territory certain southern elements of the tribe of Benjamin.

A glance at the map shows that the territory of Israel was clearly more extensive and was far richer agriculturally, while the land in Judah, generally speaking,

---

[2] The Bible sometimes calls them Ephraim. He was Jacob's son and the ancestor of one of the most powerful northern tribes. It also calls them *House of Joseph;* Ephraim and Manasseh, the two tribes descended from these sons of Joseph, exerted the leading influence in the general policy of the northern group.

was inclined to be rocky, barren, and in places a wilderness.

On the other hand, as an ethnical group the people of Judah, closely concentrated round their capital city of Jerusalem, the political and religious centre of their country, were deeply attached to the house of David. They were thus a more closely knit and homogeneous body than the federation of the Ten Tribes of Israel, which from the very beginning of their history showed a restless and on occasion a rebellious tendency.[3]

Palestine at the time of the schism (931 B.C.)

This is the kingdom established by David with care and diplomacy (in about the year 1000) which was now cut in two. Rehoboam, Solomon's son and heir, had clumsily offended the northern group of Israel, which then decided to return to independence. Henceforward there were two States: in the north, the kingdom of Israel (ten tribes) with its capital finally at Samaria; in the south, the kingdom of Judah (two tribes only) with its capital Jerusalem. All the misfortunes we shall see befalling the People of God had their political origin in this deplorable schism.

Jeroboam decided to establish his capital at Shechem, advantageously situated in the very centre of the country. Shortly afterwards, for strategic reasons, the new king moved his seat of government to Penuel on the Jabbok in Transjordania. Finally he settled at Tirzah (1 Kings 14:17). to the east of Samaria.

A curious sidelight is furnished by the fact that for the

[3] A numerical example will illustrate this point: during the two centuries which occurred between the accession of Jeroboam (931) and the Assyrian destruction of the kingdom of Israel (721) there were nineteen kings in succession, and half of them met their deaths as a result of palace revolutions; thus dynastic changes were effected by violence. In Judah, however, (capital: Jerusalem) the legitimist principle was never called in question. During the same period there were only nine kings, all of the house of David.

CYPRUS

MEDITERRANEAN SEA

• Hamath

Arvad •

PHOENICIA

Byblos
(Gebal)
(Beirut)

• Riblah

Sidon •

Damascus •

Tyre •

Acco •

Mt. Carmel

Dor •

Jezreel •

Megiddo •

Samaria •

(Tel Aviv) •

Bethel •

Ashdod •

Ashkelon •

Gath •

Jerusalem •
Hebron •

Lachish •

Beersheba •

KINGDOM OF ISRAEL

PHILISTINES

KINGDOM OF JUDAH

Gilgal •

Penuel •

AMMON

• Ashtaroth

MOAB

ARABIAN DESERT

EDOM

defence of the country (the construction of strongholds), and the building of the royal palace, Jeroboam was obliged to re-establish the system of forced labour. Thus the Israelites who had previously rebelled against Solomon's impositions and separated from Judah, were once more obliged to labour at the royal building sites.

Israel and Judah: the religious schisms (1 Kings 12:26–33; 2 Chron. 11:13–17)

At the accession of Jeroboam Israel possessed no religious capital. For some time past, it is true, the men of the Ten Tribes had sacrificed on the 'high places' venerated by tradition. There were two principal centres: Dan at the extreme north of the country and Bethel in the south. Jeroboam decided to revive these two places of pilgrimage to take the place of Jerusalem as a religious centre, since this was situated in enemy country. Henceforward it was forbidden for any of the Yahwists of the country to travel to the Temple built by Solomon in the heart of the city of David. *'You have been going up to Jerusalem long enough,'* Jeroboam proclaimed. And to encourage his subjects to worship Yahweh within the confines of Israel he added: *'Here are your gods, Israel; these brought you out of the land of Egypt!'* In each of the sanctuaries of Dan and Bethel the statue of a golden

---

PALESTINE AT THE TIME OF THE SCHISM (931 B.C.)

This is the kingdom established by David with care and diplomacy (in about the year 1000) which was now cut in two. Rehoboam, Solomon's son and heir, had clumsily offended the northern group of Israel, which then decided to return to independence. Henceforward there were two States: in the north, the kingdom of Israel (ten tribes) with its capital finally at Samaria; in the south, the kingdom of Judah (two tribes only) with its capital Jerusalem. All the misfortunes we shall see befalling the People of God had their political origin in this deplorable schism.

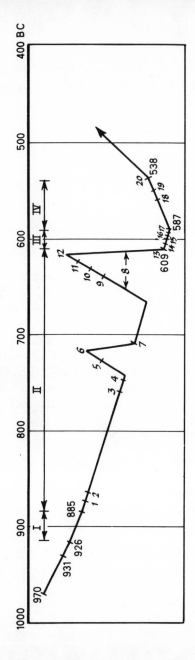

GRAPH OF THE SPIRITUAL PROGRESS OF THE CHOSEN PEOPLE
from the death of Solomon (931) to the return from the Babylonian Exile (538)
(For the periods preceding this graph, the reader could refer to the graph included in 'Solomon the Magnificent', in this series, page xiv.)

931   Death of Solomon. The schism.

931–926   Israel and Judah, enemy brothers.

I 926–885 **First blow: the Egyptian invasion.**

II 885–609 **Second blow: the Assyrian invasion.**

1. The prophet Elijah.
2. The prophet Elisha about (859).
3. The prophet Amos.
4. The prophet Hosea.
5. The call of the prophet Isaiah (about 740).
6. The time of Isaiah (740–700).
7. The capture of Samaria by Sargon II of Assyria; deportation (and dissolution) of the Ten Tribes of Israel.
8. The time of Josiah (640–609).
9. The prophet Zephaniah (about 630)
10. The call of Jeremiah (627).
11. Discovery of the Book of the Law, in Temple (621).
12. First production of the Books of Joshua, Judges, Samuel and Kings.
13. Death of Josiah on the battle-field of Megiddo (609).

III 609–587 **Third blow: the Chaldaean invasion.**

14. The revolt of Jehoiachin against his sovereign Nebuchadnezzar, king of Babylon. First deportation to Babylonia, 597.
15. The prophet Jeremiah.
16. In Babylon, to where he was deported in 597, the prophet Ezekiel predicts the destruction of Jerusalem.
17. The revolt of Zedekiah, king of Jerusalem, against Nebuchadnezzar. Fall of Jerusalem: the burning of the city. The destruction of the Temple. Second deportation (587) and third (582/581 B.C.).

IV 587–538 **Exile of the people of Judah in Babylonia.**

18. Cyrus, king of the Medes and Persians (549).
19. The anonymous prophet called 'Deutero-Isaiah'.
20. The decree of Cyrus (538). End of the Exile.

calf was set up in the place of honour on the altar. Jeroboam's idea was that they should make up for the absence of the Ark of the Covenant.

It was true nonetheless that images of this kind constituted a serious danger to the people's spiritual advancement. At this time they were already beginning to be attracted again by the Canaanite rites. In addition, the more primitively-minded of the population, and there was a considerable number of them, were incapable of distinguishing between Baal and Yahweh, between worship of the bull (the pagan fertility symbol) and the worship to be given to the holy, invisible and almighty Creator.

One result of this religious change was that the majority of the priests and levites, who served the various sanctuaries in Israel, vehemently rejected the intrusion of the idols into Yahweh's sanctuaries. And so they left Ephraim to fall back on Jerusalem. Who was to take their place in Israel? Jeroboam *appointed priests from ordinary families who were not of the sons of Levi*. This was hardly likely to augur well for the moral level of the new priestly class.

In an endeavour to minimize the consequences of the schism Jeroboam emphasised that he had no intention of breaking with traditional Yahwism. Thus he retained the great annual feast of Tabernacles, which took place in the seventh month at the Temple of Jerusalem; he made efforts to surround it with royal ceremonial, but he fixed it in the eighth month. Despite these measures the schism soon became a painful reality and a very serious matter for the spiritual future of the People of God.

The situation was made more serious still because in the south in the kingdom of Judah, under Rehoboam, the religious position was scarcely any better. Naamah, Solomon's wife and Rehoboam's mother, was an

Ammonitess, and we know that Solomon had allowed her to put up a temple to her national idols on the slopes of the Mount of Olives. Then there was Maacah (daughter or grand-daughter of Absalom), Rehoboam's favourite wife who was half Aramaean; she had been allowed to set up within the palace, and therefore close by the Temple, an altar dedicated to the impure Astarte (2 Chron. 15:16).

In addition at this period, in Judah as in Israel, there was a revival of the cults on the 'high places', as the 'high hills, shaded with green trees' were called; at one time here the Canaanite ceremonies had taken place. Since the coming of the sons of Jacob to the Promised Land these high places had gradually been transformed into Yahwist sanctuaries in which sacrifices were offered to Yahweh. But, either because the Canaanite worship had never been completely eradicated, or because gradually it had crept back on the mountains, at the period with which we are concerned we find the worship of Yahweh existing side by side with old Canannite pagan customs. Thus beside the altar of incense stood 'raised stones', sacred steles *(massaboth)*, or menhirs which, following the locality in which they stood, had different forms; in some places rounded, in others square or shaped like pyramids. These blocks of stone were regarded by the people in primitive times as the dwelling of a god *(bethel – beth*, house and *'El,* god). To feed them, or at least to worship them, libations of oil or wine were poured over them.

Another religious element that the archaeologists have discovered on the high places of Judah and Israel is the *asherah* which is mentioned angrily in the Bible from time to time. This was the 'sacred trunk', a relic of former days when the Semitic shepherd worshipped trees as the dwelling place of a female deity. A little later the *asherah* was identified with the Phoenician Astarte, the goddess of love and fertility.

Very often the staff of the high places included 'sacred' male and female prostitutes.

At the temple in Jerusalem the priests certainly did their best to preserve the law of Moses in all its purity. But high society of the capital (officers, officials and rich merchants) made a point of displaying an amused and polite disbelief. The ordinary country people were principally attracted by the Canaanite rites; increasingly they abandoned the lofty Yahwist religion to return to idolatry, a form of religion that appealed to their sensual nature and gave play to their basest instincts. Very rapidly they were coming to forget all about the Decalogue, the foundation of all civilization.

Guerilla warfare between Israel and Judah (931–926; 1 Kings 14:30; 2 Chron. 12:15)

There were no pitched battles but only skirmishes and frontier incidents – a sort of permanent state of grumbling hostility. Rehoboam nevertheless gained control of the southern part of the territory of Benjamin in order to lessen the threat to Jerusalem which was too near the demarcation line. Rehoboam confined himself to this one campaign.

In these skirmishes, which were almost continuous, the two puny States gradually eroded their military strength. Daily they wore themselves out in fruitless battles which led to no definite result. Formidable and merciless invasions by their powerful neighbours were soon to show them the futility of their stupid quarrels.

3

FIRST SERIOUS BLOW: THE EGYPTIAN INVASION

David and Solomon had been specially favoured by events outside the country: in their times, and for more than a century, the frontiers of the 'united kingdom' of Judah-Israel had not been threatened or attacked by the great military States on its borders to the south (Egypt) or the north (Mesopotamia). This is explained by the fact that from the end of the New Empire (about 1085) the power of the pharaohs was greatly weakened by internal struggles; in addition they had to defend the country against the continual attacks of the Libyans, east of the Delta. The formidable empires of Asia Minor and Mesopotamia had either, like the Hittites, disappeared from the field of history or else, like the Babylonians, had worn themselves out in military actions against their immediate neighbours. And Assyria had not yet appeared on the horizon.

Now in 925, seven years after Solomon's death, Egypt, after long being dormant, suddenly awoke with a firm intention of continuing the imperialist policy of the pharaohs of the eighteenth and nineteenth dynasties. This included expansion to the north, the domination of Palestine and dreams of conquering the countries of the Euphrates. Henceforward the kingdoms of Rehoboam and Jeroboam could look forward to heavy attack since the Egyptian army had just been thoroughly reorganized.

Sheshonk I, a grasping soldier

In about 950, shortly before Rehoboam's accession, the twenty-third Egyptian dynasty appeared. Its founder, Sheshonk I (he is called Shishak in the Bible), was a former leader of Libyan mercenaries; he was a man of energy and ambition who had little difficulty in toppling the figurehead pharaoh in whose service he was. His capital was Bubastis in the Delta.

Sheshonk it will be remembered, had eagerly welcomed the Ephraimite Jeroboam, the agitator who had tried to raise the standard of revolt against Solomon. But as he was too weak to maintain the struggle against Solomon, Jeroboam, to save his own skin, was obliged to take refuge in the Delta. Sheshonk was pleased to make him welcome. This incident gives us a fairly accurate idea of the Egyptian monarch's attitude to the king of Judah.

Sheshonk's campaign against Judah and Israel

In 925 Sheshonk launched an attack against Canaan. Rehoboam had strengthened his fortresses on his southern frontiers: Lachish and Azekah (2 Chron. 11:5–10), but in the face of the irresistible impact of the Egyptian armies the Judaean defences crumbled like straw. Sheshonk's campaign soon turned into a military progress. The land of Judah was laid waste. To avoid worse consequences Rehoboam was obliged to become the vassal of Egypt, and as such had to pay a heavy tribute. The conqueror demanded the wealth that had been accumulated in the Temple and in the royal palace. He also seized the famous golden shields which adorned the Hall of the Forest of Lebanon (2 Chron. 9:15–16).[1]

After his complete victory over Judah, Sheshonk immediately fell upon Israel despite the former friend-

[1] See preceding volume in this series, *Solomon the Magnificent*, p. 86.

20

ship, of a very fragile and purely political nature, he had shown to Jeroboam when the latter took refuge in the Delta to flee from the wrath of Solomon. Under the tide of invasion the northern kingdom collapsed as rapidly as that of the south.

We are accurately informed about these two expeditions by two inscriptions in which Sheshonk relates his exploits at length.

In the first place, at Thebes, egyptologists have discovered an enormous bas-relief on one of the walls of the great temple of Karnak. Pharaoh, the conqueror of the sons of Jacob, is depicted in a victorious attitude. He has seized prisoners by their hair and he is raising his sword to decapitate them. Behind him Amon-Ra, the god of this sanctuary, is leading to him a crowd of prisoners, of pronounced semitic appearance with their hands tied behind them. Above this procession an inscription in hieroglyphs informs us of the origin of these prisoners: *Iouta malek,* the king, or rather, the people of Judah.

On another wall of Karnak is inscribed the list of the cities which Sheshonk had just captured. There were a hundred and fifty of them, a hundred in Judah and fifty in Israel.[2]

This Egyptian conquest is proved historically by the discovery of a stele at Megiddo, a strategic point on the plain of Jezreel in the land of Israel. This stele bears the name of the victor in the great battle which took

[2] It should be noted that the Bible says nothing of the Egyptian invasion of Israel. The scribes of Jerusalem had good reasons for this. The Book of Kings, like the Book of Chronicles, was drawn up by Judaean chroniclers who frequently showed their antipathy for the kingdom of Israel and its schismatic sovereign Jeroboam. Thus they account for the Egyptian invasion of Judah by an appeal from Jeroboam who, according to them, invited Sheshonk to undertake this armed intervention. To avoid contradicting themselves they were careful not to mention the Egyptian invasion of Israel. Obviously, they could not foresee that later historians would discover the Egyptian bas-reliefs mentioned above; these provide a complete account of events. It should be added that Sheshonk did not need any suggestion from Jeroboam to return to the traditional policy of the Egyptian sovereigns for the vassalization of Canaan.

place at Megiddo. It reads, 'Sheshonk, king of Egypt'.

In addition, it is very probable that this same Sheshonk also made a special effort in the direction of Ezion-geber, the port which was established by Solomon on the shores of the Red Sea. We know that this sea had to remain an 'Egyptian lake'; that was one of the invariable points of Egyptian policy as pursued by most of the dynasties.

Sudden halt of the Egyptian invasion

This Egyptian invasion could only be regarded as the beginning of a larger campaign. Sheshonk, a clever tactician, was almost certainly planning the conquest of Mesopotamia, at this time an easy prey by reason of its political decadence and military weakness. For the Egyptian sovereigns Palestine was never anything more than a secondary objective – a sort of corridor connecting the two great States of the Middle East.

Now, quite unexpectedly, Sheshonk halted his vast undertaking. Serious revolts had just broken out in Egypt and he was compelled to evacuate Canaan, though he was careful, nonetheless, to keep a bridgehead at Gerar on the southern frontier of Judah. In fact, neither he nor his immediate successor was able to carry out the ambitious plan of campaign that he had formed. By a providential stroke of luck the Egyptian danger ceased. Judah and Israel emerged from this experience without too serious damage.

After the Egyptian invasion: twenty-five years of internal war between Judah and Israel (911–886)

The Egyptian invasion ought to have served as a salutary warning to the two small Yahwist States. In fact they left entirely out of account the terrible dangers which were beginning to appear on all sides. Instead of regrouping their forces, or of uniting in order to show a common front to invaders, Judah and Israel continued to attack each other, to tear themselves to pieces and to weaken each other. It was indeed, political suicide.

In addition, at this period a turbulent Aramean people had established themselves as a kingdom in the Damascus region. For the twenty-five years following Sheshonk's invasion of Palestine an almost uninterrupted succession of skirmishes, attacks and battles broke out between these three groups. Alliances were formed and broken off, with no positive result save for the gradual erosion of the vital strength of the opposing parties.

Obviously, this was all preparing the ground for the warlike nations of the East, for Assyria in particular, whose monarchs, eager for conquest and battle, dreamt of extending their empire from the delta of the Tigris and the Euphrates to the valley of the Nile, including Phoenicia and the land of Canaan.

Israel and Judah might well expect to pay dearly for the lack of political perspicacity on the part of their rulers.

4

THE ASSYRIAN INVASION AND THE DESTRUCTION OF THE TEN TRIBES OF ISRAEL (885–721)

This is one of the most confused periods in biblical history. During it the kingdom of Israel continued on the way to its complete and definitive downfall. The tragedy falls naturally into two distinct phases.

In the first period (885–734, that is, a century and a half), despite a marked religious decline, the development of a fine civilization can be observed. There seemed to be great hopes for the future if the formidable Assyrian threat had not already been taking shape on the banks of the Tigris.

The second phase is much shorter, lasting scarcely twelve years (734–721). The Assyrians launched a fierce attack on Samaria, the capital of Israel; there was looting and general massacre. The few survivors were deported to parts of Mesopotamia, or to even more remote countries, where every trace of them has been almost completely lost. The Ten Tribes of the northern State disappeared for ever from the field of history.

Meanwhile, the southern kingdom of Judah, completely terrorized, humbly submitted to the occupying power. Jerusalem paid the tribute demanded by the invader. Obviously, it could only be a short reprieve.

In the circumstances it was Israel, therefore, which played the major part against the Assyrian.

First phase: the strange policy of the Kingdom of Israel (885–734)

To obtain as clear an idea as possible of this complex series of events we examine here the results of the three important policies of the period, in the spheres of economics, religion and foreign affairs.

Economic policy

In 885 Omri became king of Israel and founder of the brilliant dynasty of the Omrides. The first concern of this clever monarch was to transfer his capital to Samaria, the impregnable citadel which he strengthened with powerful fortifications, capable of withstanding the heaviest assaults. On the esplanade which crowned this height he built a fine city with imposing monuments. Following the example of Solomon, whose memory was still very much alive in Canaan, Omri imported architects and decorators from the adjoining country of Phoenicia; he had ties of friendship with Ethbaal, king of Tyre. On the other hand, Ethbaal's daughter was given in marriage to Ahab, Omri's son and heir to the throne. In Samaria, and in the great cities of his kingdom, Omri encouraged the introduction and spread of Phoenician ideas and products. The taste for vast imposing monuments prevailed among the aristocracy, the military leaders and the high officials. Thus the kingdom of Israel reached a level of luxury and refinement hitherto unknown.

Ahab (874–53), Omri's son and successor, also displayed all the attributes of a great king. His wife Jezebel brought from Phoenicia the fashion for sumptuous dress and rich furnishings. Under the influence of the royal pair Samaria and Jezreel (the secondary capital) became highly civilized centres. The young sovereign took particular pleasure in adorning the palace begun by his father; at this time he built the celebrated 'house of ivory' in which lavish use was made of this exotic material which the Phoenician craftsmen carved so skilfully.

The governing classes of the northern kingdom followed their king's example in extravagant luxury.

In 841 a change of dynasty occurred. The new king, Jehu, was a rough soldier. His accession was marked by a violent reaction against the intrusion of the Phoenician Baals which had become popular in Israel at the time of the Omrides. The first result of this was that the northern kingdom broke off relations with the Phoenician territories. And the second was the abrupt arrest of the artistic movement which derived its inspiration solely from these same Phoenicians.

Nevertheless, forty years after this abrupt change one of Jehu's descendants — his name was Jeroboam II — succeeded in inaugurating a magnificent reign which, all proper allowances being made, has been compared with that of Solomon. He was a shrewd administrator, on occasion a fearless warrior, but was intelligent enough to secure for his subjects a long period of peace. He appears to stand out above all the Omrides and descendants of Jehu by his undeniable genius.

While the kingdom of Israel was thus developing a remarkable prosperity, the kingdom of Judah continued on its uneasy course. Jehoshaphat, Omri's contemporary, had also married his son to a princess of Phoenician blood, the celebrated Athaliah, Jezebel's daughter. But her only contribution to Jerusalem was the idolatrous religion of her ancestors and none of the cultural refinement of the Phoenician countries.

At the end of the period, however, during the time that Jeroboam II reigned over Israel, King Uzziah, sometimes called Azaraiah (781–740), also inaugurated a period of peace and expansion. Under the firm government of this king the southern kingdom experienced such progress that had not been seen since the first days of Solomon's reign. At this time great fortunes were built up in Jerusalem, at least among the aristocratic classes; and in the country there was an intensive development of the great estates. But the peasants and craftsmen were reduced to slavery.

Religious policy: the emergence of prophetism

From the point of view of material civilization, therefore, all seemed to be going well.

On the other hand everything seemed to go increasingly badly for Yahwism. It might well be wondered at this moment of history if in a short time the altars of the Phoenician Baal and those of his companion, the licentious Astarte, would not prevail over the worship of the one God.

In Israel, Jezebel, Ahab's wife, boldly organized the worship of idols in the land of her adoption, and the sexual rites of the 'high places' began to flourish *on the hill shaded by terebinths and green trees*. In Judah the same process occurred under the influence of Athaliah, Jezebel's daughter. Generally speaking, the kings, while remaining officially attached to the religion of Yahweh, through weakness or indifference encouraged the pagan revival. And the populace who in the bottom of their hearts had always retained an attachment for the orgiastic rites, soon returned to practices of primitive Semitic origin.

The very existence of Yahwism was in great danger.

But suddenly a reaction occurred that was both unexpected and fierce. The defence of the one God was taken in hand by men whose smallness in numbers was balanced by the vigour of their counterattack. These 'shock troops', who thus hurled themselves into battle, are called by the Bible 'the prophets'.

27

Generally, the prophet appeared to be very surprised, terrified sometimes, by the mission entrusted to him. Very often he argued and struggled against it.

His was no easy task. To the kings he had to denounce the selfishness of the wealthy classes and the most flagrant social abuses. On occasion, the man of God was required to oppose the policy adopted by the king himself. The prophet also had to tell the priests that the Law of Moses was something more than the meticulous observance of the sacrificial liturgy. The people had to be warned away from the high places where Molech and Astarte were worshipped alongside the altar of Yahweh.

The four principal prophets in the northern kingdom before the destruction of the tribes were Elijah, Elisha, Amos and Hosea.

The prophet Elijah

In about 860, towards the end of the reign of Ahab, the son and successor of Omri, there suddenly appeared the first prophet of the long line of Yahweh's spokesmen.

It has already been pointed out above that at this period the position of Yahwism was somewhat precarious: Jezebel, the king of Israel's Phoenician wife, had introduced into the kingdom the worship and priests of her gods. On the other hand Yahweh's altars were systematically destroyed (I Kings 18:30) and priests preaching the doctrine of Moses were put to death.

Elijah was a rough, violent man, as was needed in the circumstances. Clothed in a woollen mantle held at the waist by a leather belt he led a wandering existence, except during periods of meditation when he hid himself away in some wild part of the country (1 Kings 17:3–4).

We possess no biography of Elijah in the modern sense of the word; we have merely a chronicle of his achievements. In addition, for the strictly historical details the writer refers us to the 'Book of the Annals of the Kings of Israel', a well-known work of the period which, unfortunately, has not survived. So far as documentary sources are concerned we are reduced, then, to a popular account in which are jumbled together anecdotal accounts of miracles and outstanding events. All this, as is obvious, belongs not to history in the strict sense of the term but to the epic. This literary formula does not however prevent our arriving, at least occasionally, at certain valid conclusions of the greatest interest.

The text that we have presents three distinct episodes: the 'duel', of a very odd nature, arranged between Elijah and the 450 'prophets of Baal', to discover who was the true God of Israel; Elijah's mysterious journey to Sinai; and the dramatic encounter between Ahab and Elijah in Naboth's vineyard.

Jezebel, taking advantage of her husband Ahab's religious indifference, as we have just seen, started a merciless campaign against Yahwism. In answer to this persecution Elijah went to Ahab and, in the name of the one God, told him that there would be a terrible drought for three years in succession over the whole land.

While this calamity lasted (1 Kings 17–18) Elijah went to hide himself – as was only prudent – first in Transjordania and then in the land of Sidon. There he took refuge in the hovel of a poor widow and while he was there performed many miracles. Thus throughout his stay and as long as the famine resulting from the drought lasted, the widow's jug of oil was never exhausted nor the jar, in which at this period it was customary to keep meal, and this despite daily recourse to both. In addition, in dramatic circumstances, Elijah raised the widow's son from the dead.

The word of Yahweh came to him, 'Go away from here, go east-
wards, and hide yourself in the wadi Cherith which lies east of
Jordan. You can drink from the stream, and I have ordered the
ravens to bring you food there.'
He did as Yahweh had said . . . The ravens brought him bread in the
morning and meat in the evening, and he quenched his thirst at the
stream.

1 Kings 17:2–6

PARALLEL TABLE OF THE KINGS OF JUDAH AND ISRAEL
from the death of Solomon (931 B.C.) to the end of the kingdom of Israel (721 B.C.)

ASSYRIA AND EGYPT	JUDAH SOUTHERN KINGDOM	PROPHETS	DATE	ISRAEL, NORTHERN KINGDOM	PROPHETS
Blow from Egypt Sheshonk (945–925) *Blow from Assyria* Assurnasirpal II, 883–859 Shalmaneser III, 858–824	Rehoboam (931–913) Abijah (913–911) Asa (911–870) Jehoshaphat 870–848		931 900	Jeroboam I (931–910) Nadab (910–909) Baasha (909–886) Elah 886–885 Omri 885–874 Ahab 874–853 Ahaziah 853–852 Jehoram 852–841	Elijah Elisha
	Jehoram 848–841 Ahaziah 841 Athaliah 841–835 Joash 835–796		850		
Adadnirari III, 810–783	Amaziah 796–781 Uzziah 781–740		800	Jehu 841–814 Jehoahaz 814–798 Joash 798–783 Jeroboam II 783–743	Amos Hosea
Tiglath-Pileser III, 745–727	Jotham 740–736	Calling of Isaiah	740	Zechariah/Shallum 743 Menahem 743–738 Pekahiah 738–737 Hosea 732–724	
Shalmaneser V, 726–722 Sargon II 721–705			725 721	Siege of Samarias Capture of Samaria Deportation End of the kingdom of Israel	

After this period of three years the prophet presented himself before Ahab. There was a somewhat bitter exchange. Elijah then proposed to Ahab a curious experiment to demonstrate publicly who was the real God of Israel, whether it was Molech or Yahweh. For this purpose the king called together the 'four hundred and fifty prophets of Baal' on Carmel where two altars were put up — one for Baal the Phoenician, the other for Yahweh. After this Molech was to be asked to set alight the wood prepared for the holocaust. If the Phoenician god did not answer Elijah would then call on Yahweh to send fire from heaven to consume the sacrifice. The test would show which god was the real tutelary deity of the kingdom.

A colourful scene then followed. The prophets of Baal were very busy round their altar: they danced until they were tired out, they gashed their faces and cried out with all their might, *'O Baal, answer us'*. But no flame appeared. *'Call louder,'* Elijah taunted them, *'perhaps he is preoccupied or he is busy, or he has gone on a journey; perhaps he is asleep and will wake up'* (1 Kings 18:27).

At midday Elijah decided that the time for action had come. His altar was made of twelve stones, corresponding to the number of the tribes of Israel. At the prophet's first prayer the *fire of Yahweh* (lightning) *fell* on the wood of the holocaust and set it alight. *'Yahweh is God!'* the people cried in a great wave of enthusiasm. The four hundred and fifty prophets of Baal were seized and taken to be slaughtered. At once the drought ended and rain began to fall in torrents. Ahab, who was present at this imposing performance, was deeply impressed.

The massacre of the priests of Molech greatly angered Jezebel. She at once dispatched her assassins with orders to kill Elijah.

But the man of God had once more taken to flight.

Despite his resounding victory over the foreign priests he was obliged to give way in the face of naked force. Hence his profound discouragement. On Yahweh's orders he made his way to Sinai, walking *for forty days and forty nights*. All along the way he was miraculously fed by an 'angel' who brought him *a scone baked on hot stones and a jar of water* (1 Kings 19). At last he arrived on the slopes of the holy mountain where, from the mouth of Yahweh himself, he was entrusted with further missions.

Meanwhile at Jezreel, the secondary capital of the kingdom of Israel, Ahab, still fond of imposing buildings, began to erect a palace. Near the new building in course of construction was a vineyard belonging to a peasant named Naboth; the king was very anxious to establish the vegetable garden of his palace on this site, but Naboth refused to sell it (1 Kings 21:1–3). Ahab was annoyed, and Jezebel mocked her husband about it: *'You make a fine king of Israel and no mistake!'* she railed. The queen had Naboth murdered and then ironically told her husband that he could 'take possession of the vineyard that he so ardently desired: *'Naboth,'* she explained, *'is no longer alive.'*

With a glad heart Ahab went to inspect his new property. But he there came face to face with Elijah. 'You have murdered,' the prophet exclaimed angrily, 'and *now you usurp as well. For this I will sweep away your descendants and wipe out every male* belonging to your family; as for Jezebel, she shall be killed and the dogs will eat her body.' Terrified by these predictions Ahab tore his garments and put on sackcloth and humbled himself before Yahweh, but this did not prevent Elijah's prophecies from being fulfilled. (It is possible that we have here, at least for certain details, an example of *prophetia post eventum*).

In any case, Elijah took up the position of a champion of social justice, something that was not usual at the period. A century later the prophet Amos was to return to this theme and take it much further.

An assessment of the prophet Elijah's achievement can easily be made. He saved monotheism, which at this period suffered dangerous contamination from the tenets of the worshippers of Baal. Against the totalitarian paganism of Ahab and Jezebel Elijah proclaimed that Yahweh was the one God.

Are we to understand from this that the God of Elijah was universal? Certainly, and as such he was understood by the prophet. (It is true that the ordinary Israelite at that time had difficulty in admitting this, at least in his everyday life. For the full concept of the universal God we have to wait until the end of the Babylonian exile, when it was formulated by the anonymous prophet called in the Bible the 'second Isaiah' (see page 197). But the men of God were often in advance of their contemporaries.

It remains true, nonetheless, that Yahwism based on faith in the one, holy, invisible God, needed this campaign for reform if it was to survive. Indeed the whole campaign, the whole mission of this reformer is summed up in his name Elijah: *El-Yahu,* 'God is Yahweh'.

The capital importance of Elijah in the development of the religious history of Israel is brought out clearly in the New Testament in the description of the Transfiguration on Mount Tabor: On that day, St Matthew reports Jesus took with him three disciples, Peter, James and John. He moved apart from them but remained in their sight. Then suddenly *he was transfigured* and they saw him speaking with Moses and Elijah. This was obviously a symbolic conversation: Jesus, the incarnation of the new Law, beside Moses, the representative of the old Law (that of Sinai) and Elijah, the

Six days later, Jesus took with him Peter and James and his brother John and led them up a high mountain (Tabor) where they could be alone. There in their presence he was transfigured: his face shone like the sun and his clothes became as white as the light. Suddenly Moses and Elijah appeared to them; they were talking with him.

Matthew 17:1—2

personification of prophecy (Matt. 17:1–8) and traditional forerunner of the Messiah.

The Prophet Elisha (about 840–800)

Elijah was coming to the end of his career. While returning from his mysterious journey to Sinai he crossed the region of Bashan in the valley of the Jordan, and there, on a large farm he observed a young man named Elisha who was ploughing a large field. Elijah threw his goatskin cloak over Elisha's shoulders; by this ritual gesture the old prophet was showing that he had chosen his successor. At once Elisha left his plough and followed in Elijah's footsteps, hanging on his words when he preached (1 Kings 19:19–21).

A few years after this scene and under the very eyes of his disciple, Elijah was to be miraculously taken up to heaven; according to popular tradition, this took place in a fiery chariot, drawn by horses of fire in the midst of a whirlwind. Henceforward, the defence of Yahwism was laid on the shoulders of Elisha.

The story of the new prophet is still, of course, in the epic form. Here again the writer takes pleasure in relating marvellous deeds. Some of the episodes are a repetition of the marvels previously related of Elijah. It was thought right and proper to show the listener to the poem, and, later on, the reader of the chronicle that the new envoy was the genuine heir to the great prophet Elijah.

In spite of all this Elisha appears to us as a very different figure from that of his master. Elisha's ministry was usually in urban centres. While preserving his independence he remained in close contact with the few bodies of Yahwist prophets who had survived Jezebel's persecutions and who still existed in certain highly venerated religious centres, Gilgal, Bethel and Jericho.

An original side to the new prophet was his eminently

political role. The dynasty of the Omrides, far too ready to allow the Phoenician gods to be worshipped in Israel, could no longer be tolerated on the throne of Samaria. So Elisha took action. He sent one of the 'sons of the prophets' to Jehu, one of the great leaders of the royal army; Elisha's disciple poured oil over his head, declared that he was chosen by Yahweh and invested him with supreme power. He then ordered him to go and *strike down the family of Ahab . . .*, in order to *avenge the blood* of the prophets and *of all the servants of Yahweh on Jezebel and the whole family of Ahab* (see Table p. 31).

Jehu did not need telling twice; he at once set off with all speed for Jezreel where the king was. A terrible massacre then took place. Jehoram and his mother Jezebel were mercilessly butchered. Ahaziah, king of Judah, was visiting his relation just then[1]; he too was killed. Next, at Samaria, the seventy sons or grandsons of Ahab were put to the sword. Jehu finally rounded off his wholesale massacre by the systematic killing of all the upholders of the dead king and also of several of the priests of Molech.

There is no doubt that it was the survival of Yahwism that was at stake. But the methods used for this purpose appear to us to be exceedingly hasty and of inexcusable barbarity. The men who carried out the unpleasant task were uncouth and primitive; it was hardly surprising, therefore, that their bloodthirsty character was condemned by the prophet Hosea (740–720) who a century later was to herald the coming of the God of Love.

Elijah and Elisha both belong to the same epic story. But the two prophets should not be regarded as equals.

---

[1] Ahaziah of Judah married Athaliah, Jezebel's daughter and Jehoram of Israel's sister. Thus Ahaziah and Jehoram were brothers-in-law.

Elijah remains the unrivalled figure dominating the whole of prophetism.

After their death an interesting change occurred. Elijah and Elisha, who left no written works behind them, are known to us, as a matter of fact, only through an oral tradition which has embellished the fundamental theme. But after these accounts, whose uncertain and imaginative nature is sometimes to be regretted, there came the long and brilliant line of 'writer prophets' who left us a literary work which was composed by them or their disciples. And their actions occurred within a political context which endows them with undeniable authenticity. With Amos and Hosea, to begin with, we are on the firmest of ground.

The Prophet Amos (about 750)

About fifty years after the death of Elisha a strange figure appeared in the land of Israel. This was Amos, a shepherd from Tekoa (in Judah), a small village some six miles south of Bethlehem. In the spring it was his habit to go down to the plain where he was employed in tapping sycamores (Am. 7:14). He tells us the asonishing way in which Yahweh took him from herding the flock and ordered him, *'Go, prophesy to my people of Israel'* (Am. 7:15).

It was the time of Jeroboam II (783–743). Then, as has been mentioned, the kingdom of Israel experienced a period of great prosperity. The country grew in power and wealth. On the other hand, imposing ceremonies took place at the national sanctuary at Bethel. All seemed prosperous and full of hope for the future, but this was only a fine façade concealing numerous shortcomings. Actually, the great fortunes were in the hands of a single class – the royal officials and military leaders, the great landowners, merchants and moneylenders. The poorer classes were exploited without mercy. The Yahwist religion also was in the hands of a priesthood whose only concern was the strict observance of the sacrificial ritual. Thus the Judaean shepherd Amos had a twofold objective in view: he had to oppose both social oppression and the errors which had crept into Yahwism.

Amos, who was a real peasant from the wilderness, went to Bethel, the sanctuary of Israel (later, perhaps, he went to Samaria). His language was rich in powerful and vivid images as he inveighed against those in power who, in the hardness of their hearts, reduced the poor to slavery. He blamed the judges *because they have sold the virtuous man for silver and the poor man for a pair of sandals*. He denounced the mercilessness of the money lenders *who trample on the needy and try to suppress the poor of the country* by shameful speculation and falsification of measures. But what particularly enraged Amos was the insolent luxury of the aristocracy: while the peasants and the craftsmen were literally starving fine houses were built *of dressed stone* (Am. 5:11) in which there were finely-cooked meals and perfumes in profusion and orchestras to entertain the guests:

> *They bawl to the sound of the harp. . . .*
> *and use the finest oil for anointing themselves.*

But about the poverty of the people *they do not care at all* (Am. 6:4–6).

It would be wrong to look on Amos as a revolutionary leading the poor to pillage the fine houses. He merely desired that in the name of Yahweh Israel should give up its luxurious way of life and return once more to those ideals of justice befitting a worshipper of the true God.

He spoke with equal vigour against the priests. He blamed them for their formalism. He inveighed against those ceremonies in which the heart was not lifted up to God. By the mouth of his prophet Amos Yahweh thundered against the entirely external form of worship that was offered to him:

I hate and despise your feasts,
I take no pleasure in your solemn festivals. . . .
I reject your oblations,
and refuse to look at your sacrifices of fattened cattle.
Let me have no more of the din of your chanting,
no more of your strumming on harps.
But let justice flow like water,
and integrity like an unfailing stream.

(Am. 5: 21–24)

Here again we must be careful not to see in Amos a declared opponent of organized religion. Although we can detect in him a certain lack of charity, it is true nonetheless that he was a harsh critic of the way in which worship was organized in his day. He called for the urgent reform of religious practices, only too often assimilated by the priests to magic ceremonies which they thought worked automatically. The priests themselves believed that when beasts were sacrificed to Yahweh he was *bound* to protect his people and to bestow his favours upon them. Israel had lost sight of the moral character of the Covenant of Sinai and of the fact that Yahweh required, before all else, the practice of justice.

Amos proclaimed to the sons of Jacob that, despite their erring ways, they were not to think that Yahweh would protect them because they belonged to the Chosen People. Yahweh was to show himself more exacting towards them because he had chosen them from 'among all peoples'.

*'You alone, of all the families of earth, have I
    acknowledged,
  therefore it is for all your sins that I mean to punish
    you.'*   (Am. 3:2)

And punishment was on its way. While the wealthy classes in the kingdom of Israel went on their thoughtless way Amos foretold, though without actually giving it a name, the Assyrian invasion. Even then the Assyrians were making ready to engulf the country and carry out their terrible deportations of the inhabitants:

*'Listen to this word, you cows of Bashan,
  living in the mountains of Samaria,
  oppressing the needy, crushing the poor,
  saying to your husbands, "Bring us something to
    drink!"
  The days are coming to you now
  when you will be dragged out with hooks,
  to be driven all the way to Hermon.
  It is Yahweh who speaks.*   (Am. 4:1–3)

It was to be a terrible punishment. But one hope still remained: 'a small remnant' could be saved, for in regard to Israel God's plan was still in existence.

*It may be that Yahweh, God of Sabaoth, will take
    pity on the remnant of Joseph.*   (Am. 5:15)

Amos had gone too far. At Bethel, the schismatic centre of the kingdom of Israel, preaching of this kind could no longer be borne. Amaziah, the priest of the sanctuary, began to grow weary of the forebodings of this prophet of gloom. Amos would have to return home to Judah, or it would be the worse for him.

Amos was obliged to leave. His mission was over; the

shepherd of Tekoa had proclaimed that Yahweh, the Almighty, the Master of the world, required from his faithful followers a wholehearted and complete application of justice.

The Prophet Hosea (745–720)

Hosea was a native of the northern kingdom. He lived through the last years of Jeroboam II (who died in 743) and the period of anarchy which followed. It is likely he witnessed the national disaster which befell Israel, namely, the fall and destruction of Samaria (721). He was probably a contemporary of Amos.

The burden of Hosea's prophecy – the love of God – is symbolized by the tragic experience of his own marriage (Hos. 1–3). On Yahweh's orders Hosea took for his wife a prostitute named Gomer (probably a servant of the temple of Baal) who was very dear to him, but after giving him several children this woman left him to go after lovers. After great trials which crushed her Gomer returned one day to Hosea. Before resuming life together the latter demanded a period of trial in his own house; he then took her back, welcoming her with every sign of the affection which is given to the purest of brides.

There is more to these domestic details than the sorrows of Hosea's life. They are to be seen as a parable whose meaning is very moving. Making all proper allowances, we must see Hosea here as taking the place of Yahweh who had chosen Israel from among all the peoples of the earth. He surrounded her with his tender care; he 'married' the 'chosen people' for whom he had important plans, leaving them at the same time, of course, their free will. Despite some temporary lapses the Twelve Tribes seem to have accepted the lofty mission entrusted to them.

Then came the time of betrayal. Like an unfaithful

wife Israel disappointed Yahweh's hopes. She left the home to *prostitute herself to the Baals* (that is the usual expression employed by the biblical writers), she abandoned her God and returned to her old idols, she showed herself unworthy of the love of God. In this way she aroused Yahweh's anger and he made ready to punish her severely – so Hosea tells us – by the invasion of the Assyrian armies, and the laying waste of the northern kingdom.

The guilty one must show her repentance. For, despite her sins Yahweh continues nonetheless to love the faithless one. And if Israel, filled with remorse like Gomer, returns to Yahweh, he will welcome her with great love and mercy.

Hosea's message, in a few words, was this: 'God requires *love* from his creature, a love which is to be shown by the bringing into action of all the powers of the soul' (Gelin).

> *What I want is love, not sacrifice;*
> *knowledge of God, not holocausts.*

(Hos. 6:6)

Thus on the eve of the great national disaster Israel had heard:

a forceful reminder of the idea of monotheism from Elijah and Elisha;

the imperative law of social justice, proclaimed by Amos;

the revelation of a God of love and forgiveness, as portrayed by Hosea.

But this spiritual revival was still at its beginning. There were further, and more moving developments to come.

International policy: the Assyrian threat

We have seen that economically a very fine material civilization had developed in Judah.

At the religious level the result was more questionable; it looked as if in a short time worship of Baal would prevail over Yahwism. Fortunately, certain forthright prophets, real spiritual champions, entered the lists, though it must be acknowledged that only too frequently they were voices crying in the wilderness.

We must now glance at the international scene, though what we shall see gives little cause for encouragement. The situation was as follows.

On the one side there was a group of four small states: Israel and Judah, which we know already; Phoenicia, with its great ports of Tyre and Sidon; and the youthful Aramaean kingdom which had just been established in the neighbourhood of Damascus under intelligent sovereigns with disquieting territorial ambitions.

Facing this network of small nations stood Assyria, a martial empire established on the banks of the Tigris. She planned to extend her power throughout the Middle East, that is, the territory stretching from lower Mesopotamia to Egypt. The valley of the Nile, of course, was included in the list of annexations. The geographical situation involved, obviously, the invasion and subjection of Damascus, Syria and the two Yahwist kingdoms of Samaria and Jerusalem.

What was Israel's and Judah's reaction in the face of this formidable Assyrian threat?

In the first place, the Yahwist sovereigns seem to have taken the necessary counter measures. Ahab, king of Samaria, who continued the wise policy of his father Omri, formed a coalition with Israel, Judah and Damascus as members. Thus when the Assyrian king Shalmaneser III (858–824) made an expedition to the Orontes the allies presented a common front against him. At Kharkar a battle took place between the opposing forces. Shalmaneser proudly boasted in his chronicles that he won a resounding victory, though this was probably a little exaggerated. In any case, the self-styled victor seemed disinclined to continue the struggle, though it is true that, recalled to Mesopotamia by the rebellion of recently subjected peoples, he was obliged to give up his military expedition into the Mediterranean region, but was ready on the first favourable opportunity to continue his plan of campaign.

Israel and Judah realized that only a close alliance against the common enemy would save them from disaster.

Unfortunately the allies did not follow this policy for long; it was one indeed that was hardly in conformity with the ideas of the petty kings of the ancient East. As soon as the Assyrian commanders were detained by expeditions to far-off countries the small nations of Canaan quickly took advantage of this respite to attack and tear each other to pieces and to kill without mercy. Over half a century of uninterrupted warfare ensued (850–784) resulting in a general weakening of their military power while the Assyrians during this same period were perfecting their formidable war machine.

Israel, Judah and Damascus were thus preparing their own collective ruin. There is no need to recount here the whole course of the fractricidal wars in which the Assyrians lent a hand with lightning-like raids which led in the end to the plundering of Canaan, the sacking of its cities and the imposition of heavy war indemnities.

The foreign policy pursued by Israel and Judah was certainly a strange one. Their mistakes were very shortly to cost them dear.

Assyrian invasion and end of the Kingdom of Israel (734–721)

Just at this time there appeared the threat of a formidable enemy, Tiglath-Pileser III, king of Assyria, whose imperialistic ambitions included the conquest of the whole of the Fertile Crescent.

The accession of Tiglath-Pileser in 745 marks a definite turning point in Assyrian history and, consequently, in the destiny of the people of God.

He was a shrewd politician, a clever administrator and was soon seen to be an unrivalled war leader as well. He began by establishing a standing army composed of highly trained men. He reformed the fighting methods used hitherto by an appreciable reduction in the squadrons of chariots (which were unable to manoeuvre on all terrains), by increasing his forces of cavalry, by establishing strong units of pike-bearers and archers, and by providing bodies of specialist troops with formidable siege equipment.

In addition, he gave up the tactics of his predecessors, who were accustomed to return to their home bases after the systematic looting of the regions which had been temporarily invaded and in which there was no question of settling. His plan, which was quite new, consisted in the complete elimination of the opposing forces.

He was determined to spread terror everywhere so as to strike fear into the hearts of those kingdoms which dared to offer the least resistance. For this purpose, wherever an attempt was made to halt his advance by force of arms, he ravaged the countryside, burning farms, farmers and crops. After the capture of a city the Assyrian soldiers raped the women and tortured the men, impaling them on huge stakes; the defeated leaders were flayed alive and their skins stretched out on what

Tiglath-Pileser III (745–727) king of Assyria in his ceremonial chariot.
After Layard, *Nineveh and Babylon*

After the battle the Assyrian scribes calculate how many of the enemy were killed in accordance with the number of heads.
After Layard, *Nineveh and its remains*

walls were still standing. The bas-reliefs of the royal palace in Mesopotamia depict the victorious monarch feasting merrily in company with his officers; in front of the table stands a pyramid of severed heads.

The Assyrian troops no longer quitted the conquered territories after their raids as had been their practice hitherto. The kingdoms were annexed and became Assyrian provinces; they underwent occupation, for garrisons were established in them. What might remain of the native population was deported to remote countries — some three hundred or six hundred miles from their native land. Their place was taken by groups of foreigners of different language and religion who also were undergoing forced exile.

Tiglath-Pileser began by freeing Assyria from the pressure exerted by Babylon. Then he crushed the Syrian armies. In 730 he occupied Damascus for the first time. Later, he turned again on Babylon, deposed the king of this great city and himself assumed the crown under the local name of Pulu. At his death it could be said that he had set the Assyrian Babylonian dynasty well on the way to domination of the Middle East.

This was the formidable personage who was soon to make his appearance in that part of history with which we are concerned.

It was at this very time that Rezin, king of Damascus and Pekah, king of Israel, urged by Egypt, foolishly decided to take the field against Tiglath-Pileser. They thought that their coalition would be strengthened if Ahaz, king of Judah, joined them in their campaign against the Assyrians. But Ahaz (736–716) refused outright to be dragged into an adventure of this kind. Furious at this rebuff, Pekah and Rezin decided to march on Jerusalem and lay siege to it (733). Thus the Yahwist sovereign of Samaria was besieging the Holy City while the Assyrians were at the gates of Canaan; a greater blunder hardly seemed possible.

The Prophet Isaiah (740–about 700)

It was at this moment that the prophet Isaiah unexpectedly irrupted into the political life of Judah.

Isaiah's mission can be divided into three parts.

First, from 740 to 735, that is, for five years, he travelled through the country (at one time he even crossed into Israelite territory) to announce the terrible punishment that would fall on the sons of Jacob if they did not at once return to the law of Yahweh.

Then, in 735 (that is, at the beginning of the reign of Ahaz), Isaiah protested vigorously against the serious shortcomings of the king and the nation in respect of the law of Yahweh.

Lastly, in the time of Hezekiah (716–687), the son and successor of Ahaz, the prophet took charge of the affairs of Judah. But subsequently he suffered greatly when he was abandoned by the sovereign who, in the first half of the reign, had accepted the prophet's wise counsels.

Thus Isaiah's mission extended over three quite distinct periods, but the theme of his preaching remained always the same: God is mighty; we must trust not in men but in God; all things belong to God, the Master of all, the Strong One, the Holy One.

The call of Isaiah (Is. 6)

The vocation of Isaiah is related in detail in the chapter which he wrote or, at least, which he dictated to his disciples. In the year of the death of King Uzziah (that is, 740) Isaiah, priest of Jerusalem, was praying in the sanctuary. Suddenly God took hold of this man who had been meditating on the divine mysteries for many years. Isaiah was then granted an imposing vision (an interior one, very probably, of a symbolic nature) in which he saw Yahweh in all his glory, to all appearances like an eastern potentate of colossal stature. His train filled the sanctuary. The cries of the seraphs surrounding him proclaimed him as king of Israel, but also and more especially as king of the whole world. It was a mystical, transcendent vision outside time. The heralds of the Almighty flying round this apparation proclaimed the presence of God by chanting the song of praise which has been preserved in Catholic liturgy:

> *Holy, holy, holy*[1] *is Yahweh Sabaoth.*[2]
> *His glory fills the whole earth.*   (Is. 6:3)

As was pointed out above, when the prophets were told of their mission most of them, terrified by the heavy responsibilities that would fall upon them, endeavoured to refuse. With Isaiah nothing like this happened. To Yahweh's question Isaiah answered unhesitatingly and with the impetuosity of enthusiasm: *'Here I am, send me.'*

First mission: struggle against materialism and injustice (740–734)

For six years the prophet had gone round unmolested in the territory of Judah and from time to time in Israel, denouncing the scandals of the huge fortunes based on the wretchedness of the people, cursing the wealthy who wallowed in drunkenness and impurity.

> *Woe to those who from early morning*
> *chase after strong drink,*
> *and stay up late at night*
> *inflamed with wine.*

[1] Threefold repetition is a Hebrew literary device for expression of the superlative.
[2] Sabaoth: the 'God of armies'; the armies in question are those of the heavenly powers.

Nothing but harp and lyre,
tambourine and flute,
and wine for their drinking bouts.
Never a thought for the works of Yahweh,
never a glance for what his hands have done.
(Is. 5: 11–12)

Yahweh's people had turned away from him. They had betrayed him. Repentance had to enter their hearts and immediate reforms should bring back into honour that 'justice' which was the Law of Yahweh.

In the streets of Jerusalem Isaiah encountered beautiful women belonging to the aristocracy; he describes for us their ostentatious luxury which was an insult to the poverty of the people. These women were made up, and walked about affectedly. Isaiah inveighed against their display of jewelry and ornaments, the price of extortion.

The way they walk with their heads held high
and enticing eyes,
the way they mince along,
tinkling the bangles on their feet. (Is. 3:16)

There was surprise at these furious denunciations. 'Who is he getting at?' sniggered the sceptics who still had no idea of the disasters which would soon befall them. But Isaiah could see, foretell and describe them. All these beautiful women one day soon would be raped by the Assyrians; their heads with the elaborately done hair would be shaved and they would be tied together like animals; then in long lines they would have to take the road for far-off Mesopotamia.

The Lord will give the daughters of Zion itching
*   heads*
and uncover their nakedness.

That day the Lord will take away the ankle orna-
    ments, tiaras,
pendants and bracelets, the veils, headbands, foot
    chains and
belts, the scent bottles and amulets, signet rings and
    nose
rings, the expensive dresses, mantles, cloaks and
    purses, the
mirrors, linen garments, turbans and mantillas.
Instead of scent a stink;
instead of belt, a rope;
instead of hair elaborately done, a shaven scalp;
and brand marks instead of beauty. (Is. 3:18–24)

Actually, all these prophecies were fulfilled point by point in time. And Isaiah is untiring in repeating the reasons for this terrible punishment promised by Yahweh:

When you stretch out your hands.
I turn my eyes away.
You may multiply your prayers
I shall not listen.
Your hands are covered with blood,
wash, make yourselves clean.
Take your wrong-doing out of my sight.
Cease to do evil
Learn to do good,
search for justice,
help the oppressed,
be just to the orphan,
plead for the widow. (Is. 1:15–17)

We find here the same kind of language as that favoured by Amos. But Isaiah was intended shortly for another role.

Isaiah's political mission
We return now to the time when Rezin of Damascus and

Pekah of Samaria marched in concert on Jerusalem to lay siege to the city, depose the king and place on the throne a creature of their own. *Then,* Isaiah tells us, *the heart of the king and the hearts of the people shuddered as the trees of the forest shudder in front of the wind* (Is. 7:2).

Ahaz, king of Jerusalem, was quite young at this time; he had been scarcely two years on the throne and was rather inexperienced. To obtain the protection of the Canaanite deities he began by sacrificing his own young son to *pass through fire* in the Valley of the Sons of Hinnom (2 Chron. 28:3). So even the royal family had gone back to human sacrifices!

After invoking idols came an appeal to the declared enemies of the people of God. Ahaz sent an envoy to Tiglath-Pileser for the purpose of presenting him with a handsome tribute made up of *the silver and gold that was found in the Temple of Yahweh and in the treasury of the royal palace.* In addition, the Judaean envoys were instructed to throw themselves at the feet of the oriental monarch, and declare in Ahaz's name: *I am your servant and your son. Come and rescue me from the king of Aram and the king of Israel who are making war on me* (2 Kings 16:7).

When he heard of the king's decision, Isaiah as a devout follower of Yahweh was, as we may well imagine, very grieved. He decided to intervene and endeavour to open the king's eyes.

Isaiah as the bearer of a message of hope

Ahaz, in company with his military leaders, was making a tour of inspection of the ramparts of Jerusalem which would have to be put in order before the arrival of the armies of Damascus and Israel. The king was at the south-west quarter of the city looking at the work in progress.

Yahweh said to Isaiah, 'Go with your son Shear-jashub, and meet Ahaz at the end of the conduit of the upper pool on the Fuller's Field road, and say to him:
  "Pay attention, keep calm, have no fear,
  do not let your heart sink . . ." '

Isaiah 7:3–4

Isaiah came into his sovereign's presence. The prophet was then about thirty years old; by the hand he led his four-year old son to whom he had given the name *Shear-jashub,* a name full of hope but implying a long preliminary period of misfortune. The name meant 'a remnant will return'.

This prophet of violent speech, the foreteller of misfortunes, was well known; the king and his leaders expected more fearful predictions. But for once they were wrong; Isaiah had a more reassuring message to deliver this time: the king, he declared, was not to worry about the opposing armies which had set out for Jerusalem. In a short time the kingdoms of Damascus and Israel would be destroyed and wiped off the map.

We shall see shortly how the prediction was fulfilled.

Isaiah concluded his message by declaring that after the destruction of Samaria there would nevertheless remain some hope for the sons of Jacob; Yahweh had announced that there would be a remnant; this referred to the small enclave of Judah. The Assyrian threat, fatal for Israel, would be turned aside from Jerusalem if Ahaz and his subjects returned to God. Otherwise, the enemy would also sweep down to Jerusalem like a devastating wave and the southern kingdom would then be reduced in its turn to a wilderness.

Ahaz, whose faith was by no means strong, took scarcely any notice of these prophecies. He continued to trust in the fortifications of his capital and the armed forces of his ally, the king of Assyria.

Isaiah and the theme of royal messianism

Before an irretrievable mistake was made Isaiah decided to try a further approach. He went to the royal palace and there made the celebrated prophecy about the sign of Immanuel. He said to the king:

> *Ask Yahweh your God for a sign for yourself*
> *coming either from the depths of Sheol*
> *or from the heights above.*   (Is. 7:11)

But the king had no intention of being dragged into religious experiences which, it seemed to him, could be of no advantage; he preferred to confine himself to human wisdom. And his refusal was not indeed without a certain shrewdness. *'No,'* he replied, *'I will not put Yahweh to the test.'*[3] On ostensibly orthodox grounds, which concealed a complete lack of faith, the king endeavoured to reject the prophet's disquieting proposal. At this Isaiah burst out that the 'sign' refused by the king would be given at once by Yahweh himself through the mouth of his prophet:

> *Listen now, House of David:*
> *are you not satisfied with trying the patience of men*
> *without trying the patience of my God, too?*
> *The Lord himself, therefore,*
> *will give you a sign.*
> *It is this: the maiden is with child*
> *and will soon give birth to a son*
> *whom we shall call Immanuel.*[4]

This solemn prophecy, expressed in clearcut language which is a distinctive mark of Isaiah's literary genius, is actually shrouded in mystery. Is it right to regard it as a prophecy of the coming of Jesus in the distant future?

To answer this question properly — and it is a somewhat delicate one — the difficulties must be examined in order.

'Maiden' and 'Immanuel' are the two terms which must be studied first.

[3] 'Do not put Yahweh your God to the test' (Deut. 6:16).
[4] This is a prophetic name signifying 'God with us'. The name is repeated by Isaiah a little further (8:8).

In the prophecy of Isaiah she who was to give birth was designated by the Hebrew word *ha-almah*. This can be translated an unmarried young girl, usually, therefore, a virgin. In actual fact in the biblical text the idea of virginity is not predominant (cf. Prov. 30:19). Also, in certain Phoenician texts of Ras Shamra this expression *almah* is applied sometimes to the goddess Anat (also called 'virgin' – *bethulah*), and sometimes to a royal wife.

We must be careful therefore not to translate *ha-almah* exclusively by 'maiden' or 'virgin'. Now this is precisely the term that is used in biblical translation in Greek *(parthenos),* Latin *(virgo)* and English *(virgin).*

The name Immanuel *(immanu-'El,* 'God with us') must not be confused with the greeting *immanu-Yah* ('Yahweh with us'). According to Isaiah it is an *'El,* that is, a God, who is to come down among us.

In addition, in the family of David, it is a guarantee that God will not forget his promises (cf. Nathan, 2 Sam. 7), namely, that 'God is with us'.

What exactly does the Immanuel prophecy reveal to us from the historical point of view?

In the first place the sex of the child. She is 'with child and will soon give birth to a *son'*. In the east the statement that a daughter had been born did not arouse much interest. Only the birth of a male was an important family event. By its fulfilment in the future this prophecy of a 'son' would be regarded as an authentic sign.

The laying waste of the kingdom by foreign nations (Assyria and Egypt) foretold that Israel must be prepared to become a battlefield. After the clash of armies the country would experience ruin and desolation, and the the land would produce only briars and thorns.

How long was this period of trials to last? *Until he* [the child to be born] *knows how to refuse evil and choose good*. That is, in accordance with the ideas prevalent in the ancient east, between seven and ten years.

Those then are the historical implications of the prophecy.

When Isaiah spoke his contemporaries could have imagined with good reason that Immanuel would appear very shortly, and very probably in the human form of the son of Ahaz (the future Hezekiah). But by the end of the eighth century B.C. this hope had for long been disappointed. Once more the question arose: who was this miracle child?

It must be pointed out here that most of Isaiah's prophecies were given in a form that was perfectly clear. And generally he foretold events that occurred within a short space of time. But this time, forsaking his usual practice, the prophet breaks new ground, using words with several meanings and full of mystery. Here the historian needs the theologian's help to solve the difficulty.

Theologians state quite clearly that we have here a messianic prophecy, not direct but indirect or, as it is called, 'typical' or spiritual.

For the believer looks on the Bible as written by authors 'inspired' by God. God must be regarded as the originator of the Bible though this in no way prevented the writer from putting forward the facts as a man of his own time and race. Nevertheless, theologians consider that in some passages of Scripture God 'prepared applications and developments of which the human author had no knowledge. God could cause the writer to choose a word or describe events to which he intended subsequently to give new meanings from the pen of other writers at later stages of Revelation' (P. Benoit, *Initiation biblique*, p. 29). It is interesting to compare Procksh's conclusion with the passage quoted above: 'If we examine prophecy as a whole from an exegetical point of view there emerges an interpretation which is far and away superior to the confusion of opinions; it is that given by Matthew who sees the prophecy of Immanuel fulfilled in Jesus. It is true, indeed, that Isaiah does not foresee the historical figure of Jesus; as a matter of fact his vision remains in a sort of semi-darkness filled with foreboding and he himself expected the birth of Immanuel to occur very shortly. But, leaving this aside, Immanuel is really a miraculous child, the result of a miraculous birth. He is the very opposite spiritually to the worldly king. By his name he guarantees fellowship with God of the faithful remnant in which there grows a new People of God while the old perishes in the storm. We have here a messianic prophecy of the first order, the time of the birth of the image of the Messiah special to Isaiah' (*Jesaica* I, pp. 124–5).

In addition it may be wondered whether at a later date Isaiah did not have some idea of the implications of his mysterious message; for example, when he comes to the point of speaking of the messianic child who, one day, will come to give peace and justice on this earth, he does so almost in plain terms. In what is called the Epiphany prophecy Isaiah says:

> *For there is a child born for us,*
> *a son given to us*
> *and dominion is laid on his shoulders;*
> *and this is the name to give him:*
> *Wonder-Counsellor, Mighty-God,*
> *Eternal-Father, Prince-of-Peace.*   (Is. 9:5)

And also in the prophecy of the coming of the virtuous king:

> *A shoot springs from the stock of Jesse,*
> *a scion thrusts from his roots:*

on him the spirit of Yahweh rests,
a spirit of wisdom and insight,
a spirit of counsel and power,
a spirit of knowledge of the fear of Yahweh.
(Is. 11:1–2)

Now at this period the prophet Micaiah (Micah) also made a messianic prophecy in the same sense as Isaiah's. In the circumstances, 'she who is to give birth' could designate Bethlehem (which was to be the place of Christ's birth) symbolized by a woman:

But you (Bethlehem) Ephrathah,
the least of the clans of Judah,
out of you will be born for me
the one who is to rule over Israel;
his origin goes back to the distant past,
to the days of old

Yahweh is therefore going to abandon them
[Israel]
till the time when she is to give birth gives birth.
(Micah 5: 1–3)

Today exegetes accept that in the time of Isaiah and Micaiah the coming of Immanuel was beginning to become a commonplace of prophecy, firmly anchored in the history of the time. Perhaps in it may be seen the echo of an older revelation.

In any case the messianic character of these prophecies is confirmed by the apostle Matthew (1:23); and he could not be regarded as an innovator. Already Jewish tradition recognized the prophetic character of these statements. There is proof of this in the biblical translation known as the Septuagint (third century B.C.) in which the Hebrew term *ha-almah* is translated by the Greek word *parthenos* (virgin).

To conclude this brief intrusion into theology, it should be pointed out that the Church has defined nothing on the subject of the biblical texts which we have just examined.

Isaiah's apparent failure and temporary retirement from public life

Ahaz, king of Judah, was quickly exasperated by this fiery preacher continually returning to the charge. He felt that he had enough to do and to worry about with the anti-Assyrian coalition opposing him and the defensive alliance which he was trying to negotiate with Tiglath-Pileser. In consequence, the palace door was very soon closed against the insufferable prophet.

In desperation Isaiah turned to the good people of Jerusalem. He inveighed publicly against the government and its religious policy. He gave out that Damascus and Samaria, whose armies at that very moment were advancing on Jerusalem, were not to be feared. Damascus would shortly be destroyed and Samaria would be captured. Far more formidable, in fact, was the Assyrian army of 'liberation' (as it was called) which had just been summoned by Ahaz. It was the so-called ally who would lay waste Judah and reduce it to slavery and set up its own god Asherah on the holy rock in Jerusalem.

To convince his fellow-citizens and co-religionists Isaiah had no hesitation in using the most picturesque and spectacular methods. But he obtained only a very relative success due to curiosity. He then began a campaign with well-chosen political slogans, but they were no more successful.

Isaiah was deeply discouraged and bewailed the blindness of the kingdom:

A sinful nation, a people weighed down with guilt,

a breed of wrong-doers, perverted sons.
They have abandoned Yahweh.

Rejected by the king and jeered at by the people, Isaiah decided to withdraw from public life. Surrounded by a few devoted disciples determined to continue the work of reconstruction after the disaster, the prophet gave up the struggle for the time being. For eighteen years (734–716) he kept silence; for him it was a long period of study, meditation and waiting in sadness. In a later chapter we shall encounter him again, fiery as ever, at the accession of Hezekiah (716) whose trusted counsellor he became, a sort of prime minister, enjoying the king's confidence and conducting the temporal concerns of the country in accordance with the Law of Yahweh with remarkable clearness of vision and shrewdness.

Tiglath-Pileser defeats the enemies of Ahaz, king of Judah (734–732)

At the beginning of hostilities Judah faced attack from three sides. From the north the country was assailed by the allied armies of Damascus and Israel, from the south by Edom and from the south-west by the Philistines. But at this point Tiglath-Pileser's Assyrian army began to move in answer to Ahaz's appeal. The formidable steamroller was ready to crush everything in its path. In three successive campaigns the Assyrians were able to quell the trouble-makers.

734. Tiglath-Pileser went down the coast of Canaan to deal with the Philistines. At Gaza he established a garrison which in the end kept the Egyptians in check.

733. Tiglath-Pileser attacked Israel, laid waste the country to the north, deported part of the populations of Galilee and Transjordania, razed Megiddo and Hazor to the ground. But he did not yet attack Samaria.

732. Damascus was besieged and capitulated. King Rezin, the instigator of the coalition, was killed.

In Israel Samaria had still to be captured before the annexation of the little which remained of the rest of the territory, that is, Ephraim and a part of Mannaseh. It was easy to see that Tiglath-Pileser would have little difficulty over this. Now, contrary to expectation, Samaria was to escape for the time being. A clever usurper (called Hosea, not to be confused with the prophet mentioned above) took command of the movement of insurrection, murdered the unfortunate and incapable Pekah, seized the crown of Israel and lost no time in declaring himself the humble and obedient vassal of the Assyrians. In these circumstances Tiglath-Pileser agreed to leave this figure-head on the throne since, in reality, Israel now became an Assyrian province.

It looked as if Ahaz's diplomacy had succeeded, but it had not done so by any means.

Tiglath-Pileser's harsh treatment of his ally Ahaz, king of Judah

At Jerusalem Ahaz was not long in reaping the reward of his colossal political blunders. Yet with his usual bluntness Isaiah had warned him very clearly. Everything feared by the prophet, all the misfortunes and the rest which he had foretold, were to come to pass one after the other.

First came the loss of freedom for the kingdom of Judah, which the Assyrian ruler placed on the same level as the conquered nations, taking no consideration of its former status as an ally and friend. Tiglath-Pileser was then occupying Damascus, which he had recently captured. He summoned Ahaz who was called upon to swear fidelity to his new overlord. Ahaz had also to pay over a very large sum in tribute.

A deadly affront was then offered to the religion of Yahweh. Ahaz was obliged to bow down before the Assyrian deities; he prostrated himself, burned his holocaust and poured a libation. In addition in Jerusalem he built an altar to a Mesopotamian god, which stood in front of the sanctuary of Yahweh. The great altar of bronze, set up by Solomon in this place of honour, was moved to the side of the Temple. Despite the obscurity of the text (obviously the writer of the book was reluctant to go into details about these wicked changes) it seems fairly certain that some images of Assyrian gods were set up in the Temple itself; the considerable 'purification' which a few years later king Hezekiah was obliged to carry out seems to show that some very strange guests had found a place in Yahweh's Temple. In addition, on the high places worship of the Baals flourished.

We do not know exactly how Isaiah, who had withdrawn to a secret hiding-place, judged these deplorable events. It is not difficult to imagine the great grief which they caused him.

Thus this reign, disastrous on all counts, went on, yet in spite of everything, Jerusalem and Samaria, the capital cities, were still standing. But they did not last long. Samaria was the first to disappear in appalling circumstances.

Hosea, the king of Israel's double game (734–724)

To restore his kingdom, Hosea, the new sovereign of Samaria, had only to await one of the frequent reversals of fortune experienced by the Assyrian empire which, although powerful by reason of its extensive nature, was weak at its base.

Just then Shalmaneser succeeded Tiglath-Pileser on the throne of Nineveh. While ostensibly professing complete submission to his Assyrian overlord, Hosea plotted with So, the king of Egypt. It appears that Hosea's machinations had been reported to Shalmaneser who, like all despots, was heavy-handed: Hosea was arrested immediately, thrown into prison and bound in chains. We are not told what fate awaited him but there seems little doubt about it.

This was a favourable opportunity for Assyria to wipe from the map this tiny vassal kingdom whose frontiers had been eaten into considerably by recent annexations. The destruction of Samaria was to be the salutary lesson administered to rebels who endeavoured to join forces with Egypt. Without delay Shalmaneser invaded the much diminished territory of Israel and laid siege to Samaria (724).

The siege of Samaria, 724–721 (2 Kings 17)

Although without its leader, the military party of Ephraim, trusting in the strategic position and the huge fortifications of Samaria, decided to offer stubborn resistance to the Assyrian army's attack. The Egyptian pharaoh took good care not to go to the help of his Israelite ally whose cause seemed lost in advance.

Leaving a body of troops before the besieged city, Shalmaneser went on to Tyre and Sidon (where, as a matter of fact, he did not achieve the result that he expected). During this expedition to Phoenicia Shalmaneser died somewhat mysteriously. Sharukhin (Sargon II) one of his principal lieutenants, succeeded him at the head of the army and of the government of the kingdom.

The siege of Samaria took its normal course. Modern archaeologists have discovered two enclosures: a carefully constructed inner wall about four and a half feet thick, and an external enclosure of an average width of thirty-two feet with towers and fortifications. The besieging forces may well have been practised hands,

EXILE OF THE INHABITANTS OF THE KINGDOM OF ISRAEL (SAMARIA) 721 B.C.

721: Samaria, capital of the kingdom of Israel, falls into the hands of Sargon, monarch of Assyria, after a three years' siege. The conqueror lays waste the countryside and massacres the inhabitants. Part of the survivors of Samaria were deported; one group of them settled at Halah, south of Nineveh, another group was exiled in the remote country of the Medes (to the north-east of Mesopotamia). In return the region of Samaria was repopulated on the orders

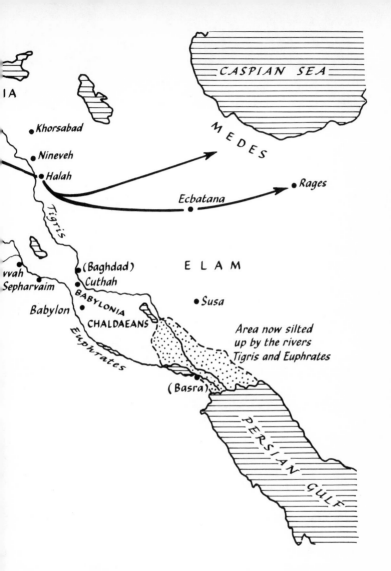

of the Assyrian government by inhabitants from Babylon whose religion was Mesopotamian, and natives of Cuthah, Avva, Hamath and Sepharvaim. These newcomers, mingled with the Israelites who had received permission to remain in their ancestral country, formed the odd religious group of doubtful orthodoxy known as the Samaritans.

nevertheless they must have found the city a difficult obstacle. Finally, at the end of the third year of siege, a heavy attack against the exhausted garrison succeeded in breaching the rampart by battering ram. Samaria, capital of Israel, fell into the hands of the Assyrians.

Capture and plunder of Samaria (beginning of 721) and deportation of the population

Sargon II appears to have been a typical merciless eastern potentate. In the Louvre Museum there is a striking and rather frightening portrait of him; seeing it we can understand how he struck fear into the whole Middle East, Egypt and Ethiopia. In addition to his military exploits he was a great builder; to the north of Nineveh he established the splendid and very large capital, Khorsabad (Dur Sharrukin).

Sargon, enamoured of fame, had the account of his exploits inscribed in various places. Here are some of the texts in which he recounts his victory. 'I besieged the city of Simirina and captured it. I deported 27,290 of its inhabitants. I took fifty chariots. The other inhabitants I allowed to keep their possessions. I appointed a lieutenant over them and demanded the same tribute as the previous king.'

On the famous cylinder known as 'Sargon's cylinder' there is a similar inscription: 'The man of Samaria who had united with a king[5], had entered an alliance not to do me homage and not to pay me the tribute; he engaged me in battle; by the power of my great gods, my lords, I fought against them: 27,280 persons with their chariots, the gods in whom they put their trust; for my royal army I seized 200 chariots.'

The cylinder provides us with summary details on the place of deportation to which the inhabitants of Samaria

[5] Probably the petty king of Hamath, or So of Egypt.

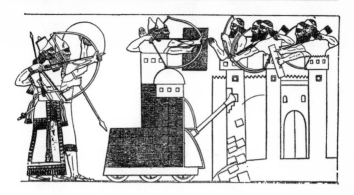

The siege of a city attacked by the Assyrians. Notice the mobile tower with six wheels armed with a battering ram.
After Layard, *Nineveh and its remains*

were sent. 'The remainder [that is, the survivors of the massacre after the capture of the city] I instructed to settle in the middle of Assyria.'

On the other hand the Bible (2 Kings 18:11), which is rather reticent about the siege of Samaria, provides more detail about the various places of deportation: 'The king of Assyria deported the Israelites to Assyria and settled them in Halah on the Habor, a river of Gozan, and in the cities of the Medes.'[6]

Such was the method of pacification introduced and largely used by the Assyrians to break down national resistance. The operation was threefold; first came the systematic massacre for the purpose of causing terror, and the destruction of the principal buildings; many prisoners were impaled, murdered, flayed alive, had their hands struck off or their eyes put out. Then those who were left of the leading inhabitants were transported to a more or less remote region. Finally, the country which had

[6] Halah, probably to the south of Nineveh. 'In the cities of the Medes': a far more remote place of deportation than the first mentioned; it is the region on the other side of the Tigris and the Zagros mountains. Here, at a later date, the story of Tobit was set.

thus been depopulated received a contingent of other deportees coming from a foreign land. This mixing of populations ensured a certain amount of tranquility to the conquerors in countries which were too turbulent.

The Assyrians obviously had no interest in reducing these exiles to conditions of extreme poverty. Usually they were allowed to take with them from their country of origin a portion of their possessions. Once they were established in their new home they were able to enjoy a certain freedom; they could farm or even engage in trade. The Book of Kings provides practically no information on the daily existence of these 'displaced' Israelites, but some idea of it can be obtained from certain passages in the story of Tobit.

The curious repopulation of Samaria

Taken as a whole, Samaria and its territory was harshly treated. The city was plundered; then, anything of commercial or artistic value was carried off to the banks of the Tigris. The former kingdom of Israel had now to be repopulated in accordance with Assyrian military practice.

The prism of Sargon relates this event as follows. 'I built [it is Sargon speaking] the city of Samaria so that it was greater than it had been before. I established there a population from countries that I had annexed by conquest. Over the country I installed my officer as governor and I incorporated this people in the administrative system of Assyria.'

The Bible (2 Kings 17:24) furnishes details which support this statement but are more precise: 'The king of Assyria brought people from Babylon, Cuthah, Avva, Hamath and Sepharvaim and settled them in the towns of Samaria to replace the Israelites; they took possession

The king of Assyria brought people from Babylon, Cuthah, Avva, Hamath and Sepharvaim, and settled them in the towns of Samaria to replace the Israelites . . . They worshipped Yahweh and served their own gods at the same time . . .

2 Kings 17:24,33

of Samaria and lived in its towns.' [7] (See map, pp. 66–67).

The Bible describes this repeopling of the northern kingdom in a rather schematic way. As a matter of fact there were several bodies of deportees sent to Samaria one after the other at intervals of some years. According to Sargon's annals the first of these operations took place directly after the fall of the capital. And according to the Book of Ezra the last arrival of deportees was in about 671 in the reign of Esarhaddon, king of Assyria.

All these very diverse elements of population, coming from different countries in the Middle East, brought with them to the former Israelite territory their local gods which they quickly set up in their new country. The city temples, like the high places in the country, were peopled therefore with idols hitherto unknown in this Yahwist land. Thus the Chaldaeans, who came from Babylon, worshipped a god called Succoth-Benot; the people from Cuthah adored Nergal, those from Hamath worshipped Ashima, those from Avva Nibbaz or Tartak. Lastly, the people from Sepharvaim burned their newborn children to draw down the blessing of their local deities Adrammelek and Anamelek.

While the newcomers still kept their own deities they could see nothing wrong in adopting in addition the religion of the country in which the Assyrians had made them settle by force. They saw no reason why they should not worship Yahweh, the protector of Canaan, as well as their ancestral gods. The odd religious mixture which this produced can be imagined. It was composed of the primitive rites preserved by the deportees, the Canaanite cults which had remained fairly strong on the high places, and the Yahwist religion. In Jerusalem men veiled

[7] Cuthah: a Chaldaean city (Chaldaean inscriptions call it Kuthi) which could be the modern Tel-Ibrahim, about nine miles to the north-east of Babylon. Avva: on the Euphrates. Hamath: on the Orontes. Before falling into the hands of the Assyrians this city resisted very strongly. Sepharvaim: a Babylonian city.

their faces before the curious pantheon in which Yahweh, the one God, was surrounded by cruel and notoriously immoral idols. It was a dreadful insult to the one God.

These barbarous settlers, established in the capital founded a century and a half previously by Omri, continued to be regarded by the Judaeans with distrustful hostility even in our Lord's time; aggressively they called them Samaritans. And in fact these Samaritans remained at a primitive stage of religious development, accounted for by their very mixed racial origins. At the end of the Babylonian Exile (538) when the Judaeans returned to the City of David, their neighbours, the Samaritans, had then become Yahwists, although certain beliefs and special rites still distinguished them from orthodox Judaism.

The end of the ten tribes of Israel (721)

The deportation of the remaining element of the northern kingdom, established two centuries previously by Jeroboam, sounded the death knell of Israel. The Ten Tribes were dispersed among crude ethnical elements of Babylon. They disappeared for ever, absorbed by the very varied elements which made up the milieu in which they were plunged. Yahwism of the north was not religiously strong enough to withstand the test of deportation. At Jerusalem only a vague memory was preserved of the various places assigned as the residence of their brothers of the north who only too often had shown hostility to Judah. In any case there was no communication between Jerusalem and the displaced populations.

It was the end of the Ten Tribes of Israel.

There now remained only the tribe of Judah (to which, to preserve the principle of the Twelve Tribes, was joined the small, almost imaginary tribe of Simeon).

At this stage of the story if may well be wondered

how long Jerusalem would remain sheltered from the great political upheavals.

5

SECOND BLOW:
THE CHALDAEAN INVASION
AND THE DESTRUCTION
OF JERUSALEM (721–587)

Of the fine kingdom established in about the year 1000 by David, after the fall of Samaria (721) three centuries later, there remained only the territory of Judah (see map, p. 12). It was in fact a very small country with a population of less than 200,000. Jerusalem was hardly any larger than a country town of some 30,000 inhabitants. This Yahwist enclave, a vassal incorporated by Assyria into its huge empire, seemed indeed very small. The empire stretched from Babylon to Mount Ararat in Armenia; from Nineveh, the Assyrian capital, to the sources of the Tigris and the Euphrates; from Cilicia and Phoenicia as far as Egypt.

Judah might chafe under the Assyrian yoke, but for the time being at least, with such derisory forces there could be no thought of her freeing herself from the burden of Assyrian occupation. Judah had no alternative but to accept her fate. The tragedy which had recently engulfed the Ten Tribes of Israel would serve as a solemn warning for the southern kingdom.

It remained to be seen whether those in power in Jerusalem were clever enough politicians to avoid the same serious mistakes which led Samaria to its fall.

Summary of the course of events

This chapter is fortunately a little less complicated than the preceding one.

First there was a strenous attempt at religious, moral and national reform under the influence of the new king Hezekiah, encouraged and advised by the prophet Isaiah. Hezekiah initiated a foreign policy which appeared to be sound enough, though at certain periods he made unfortunate mistakes.

Next there was a gap of half a century in which two insignificant and worthless kings reigned.

Then, with Josiah, we have the great reforming king who endowed Judaism with its irresistible resolution and ardour.

The third and last stage is marked by a return to the traditional mistakes; once again there was an outburst of that shortsighted nationalism which led to the confrontation of Judah and a great Mesopotamian power, but this time it was Nebuchadnezzar, king of Babylon, who made sure of victory.

The Babylonians swiftly secured the defeat of Judah, the capture of Jerusalem, the sacking of the city, the destruction of the Temple built by Solomon to the glory of Yahweh, and finally the deportation of the pick of the population of Judah to the banks of the Euphrates.

The Israelite kingdom of Samaria had disappeared for ever; its deported population amalgamated with the local inhabitants, and the Assyrian government re-populated the northern kingdom with racial groups from remote regions. Thus Israel was no more than a name; its religion was no more than a memory.

Now, in 587, one hundred and thirty years after the northern kingdom the Judaean kingdom of Jerusalem disappeared in its turn, but under very different conditions. During their exile in Babylon a section of the deported population from Jerusalem managed to preserve the memory of their country of origin; they retained their own identity and, more important still, their faith in the one, holy and invisible God. We find them clinging quite astonishingly to the Yahwist religion, which was to be purified unexpectedly despite the pagan and dissolute character of the society in which it was plunged. In the Babylonian crucible, where the deported population were to experience the harsh moral trials of exile, far from the land of their fathers, Judaism began to be formed. And thus, after five centuries of continual spiritual wandering, was opened the path which was to lead to the threshold of the revelation of the Gospel.

With the harsh blow from Babylon and the destruction of Jerusalem — an insignificant episode from the viewpoint of the great empires of the period — we come to one of the most moving pages of the spiritual history of mankind.

1. The great reign of Hezekiah (716–687)

In 716 Ahaz, the unbelieving king, died. His son Hezekiah (he was twenty-five years old and was to reign thirty years) succeeded to the throne of Judah. In Jerusalem people began to realize how great had been the blunders of the late king.

Hezekiah immediately reversed the distressing policies of his father; he made ready to work with all his strength for the recovery of the kingdom.

The chapters devoted to him in the Bible (2 Kings 18–20; 2 Chron. 29–32) might well give the impression that Hezekiah was a man of rather changeable character. Sometimes, under the influence of Isaiah, a declared supporter of a policy of peace at any price, he adopted a strong attitude of non-intervention; sometimes, when pressed by the military party, he decided to resort to arms.

In addition we observe Hezekiah carrying out far-reaching structural reforms in the principal social institutions of the country.

At first sight all this appears piecemeal, disorganized and even contradictory. Hezekiah seems to be a baffling personality by reason of his sudden changes of foreign policy. In reality he was psychologically a resister. At the beginning of his reign, because he felt that he was still too weak to attack the Assyrians, he was scrupulous in following Isaiah's directions. Just then the whole kingdom of Judah was in need of reconstruction in every way. Determined one day to confront the Assyrian colossus, Hezekiah endeavoured to gather all the living strength of the State under his command. Once he had attained his objective, and only then, he would launch an attack on the occupying power to try to free Judaean territory from the enemy.

The outstanding reforms by Hezekiah, a king who appeared to belong to the partisans of peace, were aimed at the patient renewal of the spirit of Judah to enable Hezekiah to throw himself one day on his hated enemy.

The work of renewal which formed part of the secret royal policy was many-sided; religious reform of the priesthood, moral reform of the people, historical reconstruction of the national past, the drawing up of a legislative code which was necessary to establish society on a firm basis; and, of course, the organization of the army which, when the time came, would give the signal for war.

Hezekiah's religious reform (first years of the reign)

Right at the beginning of his reign Hezekiah was very

energetic in the restoration of the authentic worship of Yahweh; this involved at the same time a reform of the priesthood.

In the first place Yahweh's Temple had to be put in order; it had been publicly profaned by the intrusion of Assyrian idols whose presence constituted an enduring insult to the Lord. Within the sanctuary there stood the bronze serpent called Nehushtan[1] (2 Kings 18:4). A questionable tradition ascribed its origin to the time of Moses (Numb. 21:9–9); according to this the leader of the Chosen People had agreed (unwillingly, it appears from the text) that the wandering tribes crossing the desert on their way to the Promised Land, should make this figure; and the Bible tells us that it was enough for any man bitten by a snake[2] to look on this metal idol to be miraculously cured. Since time immemorial Nehushtan had been enthroned in the sanctuary and the priests of Yahweh paid honour to it by burning incense before it[3]

On the orders of the young king the priests *brought out everything unclean they found in the sanctuary of Yahweh, out into the court of the Temple of Yahweh, and the Levites collected it and carried it outside into Wadi Kidron* (2 Chron. 29:16).

These revolutionary actions already enable us to perceive the new king's anti-Assyrian attitude.

Hezekiah continued his campaign of purification by demolishing the altars of *bamoth* (high places), by

[1] There is a play on words here of the kind favoured in the east: the word *nahash* (serpent) is combined with *nehosheth* (bronze).

[2] These were, very probably, horned vipers or cerastes; these snakes lie almost completely buried in the sand, and it is only with difficulty that their eyes can be made out at ground level. These snakes are still numerous today on the plains of Edom which were crossed by the nomad tribes under Moses.

[3] Archaeological excavations carried out in various places have brought to light several votive offerings in the form of a snake; at Gezer, particularly, a fine specimen some six and a half inches long dating from about 1000 B.C. In addition, at Suza, the former capital of Elam, a bronze serpent nearly ten inches long has been discovered.

throwing down the raised stones (*beth-'El*, house of God), by ordering the cutting down of the *asheras* (sacred poles), the phallic symbols stuck in the ground, and by starting a campaign of systematic destruction of idols. But it must be pointed out that except for the Temple, where the purification was carried out with meticulous care, the purification of the places of sacrifice was effected very imperfectly.

At the same time it was necessary to reform the priests who in the general national disorder had forgotten their most elementary duties.

In the name of the priesthood Hezekiah made public apology in the presence of the priests and Levites who had gathered in the eastern square of the Temple court. And then he made a public confession which was very moving indeed: *'Listen to me, Levites!'* he exclaimed. *'Sanctify yourselves now and consecrate the Temple of Yahweh, the God of our ancestors, and eject what is impure from the sanctuary. Your ancestors have been unfaithful and done what is displeasing to Yahweh our God. They have deserted him; they have turned their faces away from the place Yahweh has made his home, they have turned their backs on him. They have even closed the doors of the Vestibule* (a measure due to Ahaz, probably on Sargon's orders), *they have put out the lamps and offered no incense, no holocaust to the God of Israel in the holy place. So the anger of Yahweh has fallen on Judah and Jerusalem . . . I am now determined to make a covenant with Yahweh, the God of Israel, so that his fierce anger may be turned away from us . . . My sons, be negligent no longer, for Yahweh has chosen you to stand in his presence and serve him, to conduct his worship, and offer him incense'* (2 Chron. 29:5–11).

Eight days of ceremonies followed. And a further

eight days were necessary to prepare the fresh purification of the Temple. All the ritual objects cast out by Ahaz to comply with the demands of his Assyrian masters were brought back and the priests could thus take their places again before the altar.

Hezekiah's religious plan, coupled with certain political implications, was to centralize the worship of Yahweh in the Temple of Jerusalem by attributing to Solomon's sanctuary an important national function.

For this purpose it was decided to summon the people to the sacred rock for the celebration of the Passover. This plan took into account the possibilities for travel of those who were furthest away (the few survivors of the former kingdom of Samaria had scarcely twenty-five miles to walk to reach Jerusalem). Ever since the time of Ahaz the passover festival had been greatly neglected. It was fitting therefore in the circumstances to perform it with special magnificence and increased devotion in the Temple court.

Now the right date for the festival was already a few days past. According to the rule laid down by Moses the Passover ought to have been celebrated on the fourteenth day of Nisan (March–April). Fortunately it was allowed in case of necessity to postpone the festival to the following month (Num. 9:6–13). The king decided to summon all the descendants of Jacob, including the survivors of the northern kingdom, to come to Jerusalem to celebrate the great religious festival of Israel in which the dramatic events of the flight from Egypt were relived.[4]

Messengers were sent to all Israel and Judah *from Dan to Beersheba,* that is, from the extreme north of the country (where the Jordan rises) to Beersheba in the southern wilderness, to exhort the faithful to come on that

---

[4] In *Moses and Joshua* in this series (pp. 68–72) will be found details of this nocturnal vigil which according to the law of Moses the Jews must commemorate even today.

day to the sanctuary of Jerusalem which *Yahweh has consecrated for ever*. The conclusion of the appeal was pressing: *'If you come back sincerely to Yahweh, your brothers and your sons* (the deported Israelites) *will win favour with their conquerors and return to this land, for Yahweh your God is gracious and merciful'* (2 Chron. 30). Hezekiah's messengers thus went to *the land of Ephraim and Manasseh* and Zebulun (the former territory of Samaria) but in some places *the people laughed and scoffed at them*. Nevertheless, a good proportion of those in the former kingdom of Israel accepted the invitation in the end. Thus was effected the first step towards reunification; the principle of the reconstitution of the State of David was admitted. It seems that by mutual agreement all were endeavouring to forget the painful events which accompanied and followed the schism of Rehoboam.

From the religious as from the national viewpoint it was a shrewd policy.

Hezekiah's moral reformation

It would be wrong to judge these various religious reforms merely externally. In some sort they constituted the counterpart of a profound moral transformation. At the end of the seventh century the idea of social justice appeared, which henceforward was to be shown by the feeling of mercy, of brotherly help, and of the fellowship of the wealthy man with his less fortunate contemporaries.

The prophet Amos, as we saw (p. 38) defined this 'justice' with concrete examples, and with disquieting statements about the spiritual level of the society of the time. From certain indications to be found here and there we can see how the great fortunes were accumulated. The peasant was always at the mercy of a drought

82

or a plague of locusts; after a poor harvest he was obliged to borrow from a moneylender in order to continue. If the following year was as hard as the previous one he ran into further debt, always at a usurious rate of interest. By force of circumstances the debtor could no longer pay his debt and the lender applied for distraint on his possessions. The insolvent peasant with his whole family was then reduced to the rank of a slave and was sold as such. It was in this way that gradually the large estates came into existence. These estates were usually administered by greedy and merciless stewards, for the capitalist was very careful not to live in the country; he preferred a house in the city, where his immense income enabled him to enjoy all the pleasures of life.

Despite the cries of warning by Amos the people seem not to have understood the dangers threatening them. A little later Isaiah was no more successful. Man remained buried in his fierce egoism. It was every man for himself, with never a trace of any feeling of pity for the great mass of workers. There was never any question of brotherly actions. A man's life, it was thought, was what God gave him, it was what he deserved. No one thought of helping his neighbour, at least outside the very restricted category of his own family. Life was hard; a man was master or slave, rich or poor. It was the duty of each individual to work in his own personal sphere, and so far as he could, better his own state. Of course, the Mosaic Law exhorted the Yahwist not to forget his duty towards his brothers, but these were very ancient texts and no one appeared to take any notice of them.

The historian finds this unrelenting frame of mind still flourishing at a very much later date in the developed civilizations of Greece and Rome, and this is true of the whole course of their history. There was no respect for the human person. But these peoples of the Mediterranean had one excuse at least: they were not under the rule of the Law of Moses.

Hezekiah was alive to the danger that this iniquitous viewpoint represented for the people as a whole. Since he had determined to refashion the soul of his people to give them cohesion enough to attack the Assyrians — one day at least — he was obliged in the first place to put an end to oppression of the peasant or city artisan by the wealthy class. If Judah was to be regenerated 'justice' must reign over the People of God. And here collaboration with the prophet Isaiah proved very fruitful.

Already in the time of Amos the practice had begun of calling *anaw* (plural *anawim*) the 'poor of Yahweh', the man whom the greed and hardness of heart of the rich reduced to a distressing and often hopeless position. Thereby the victim was practically excluded from the moral and religious benefits of the Covenant proclaimed on Sinai:

> *They trample on the heads of ordinary people*
> *and push the poor out of their path,*

exclaimed the prophet Amos angrily (Am. 2:7).

A few years later Isaiah returned to the same theme, transferring the divine anathemas addressed to the grabbers of property to the merciless masters, the lying officials, the judges whose judgements could be bought:

> *By what right do you crush my people*
> *and grind the faces of the poor* (anawim)?
> (Is. 3:15)

Now this poor man, this beggar brought to his present plight by the egoism of his own people, this *anaw* appears as the friend, the dependent of Yahweh. That is the social morality that is beginning to emerge. The love of

God is withheld from the oppressor and given to the oppressed.[5]

This great moral advance was sustained and advanced by the prophets Amos, Hosea, Micah and Isaiah, but it was Hezekiah who nonetheless remained its architect in the social field.

The literary and religious role of Hezekiah's 'academy'

The expression 'the century of Hezekiah' has sometimes been used, in reference at least to the literary activity of the period. The term is accurate enough, and it has the merit of emphasizing the decisive role of the king of Jerusalem in the literary field at this period of ancient history which, in both style and inspiration forms the Hebrew classical period.

It should perhaps be recalled here quite shortly that at the time of Solomon in the first place, and then shortly after his death, two important historical works were produced – the Yahwist cycle and the Elohist cycle.[6]

In Solomon's reign a group of writers (priests of the Temple, and also the royal scribes) thought it their duty to collect and write down the oral traditions about the important events of national history. It was true that the memory of the professional story-tellers was to be relied upon, and although the stories were in oral form they were passed on comparatively unchanged. Nevertheless, there was some danger of their being lost since the

[5] Shortly, the term *anaw* was to take on a wider religious meaning. From its purely sociological meaning at first it then evolved to a spiritual sense. Soon the *anaw* was no longer to be a beggar, a slave, a proletarian, but the faithful Yahwist intent on putting the word of God into practice. The *anaw* was always striving to discover what study of the Law would reveal to his heart. So we can observe the emergence of a really spiritual religion which henceforward came to be imperative for man who had hitherto been too much concerned with the meticulous performance of ritual. Here we come to a turning-point of great importance in the history of the spiritual progress of humanity.

[6] For a more detailed explanation see *Solomon the Magnificent* (pp. 133–134) in this series. The genesis of these two works is there described; at a later date they were joined together in one.

continuity of this form of documentation was too closely bound up with the survival of a small group of professionals. That is why in Solomon's time it was thought prudent to record in writing the principal chapters of national history. In this way appeared the work known to biblical scholars as the 'Yahwist cycle' (God is called 'Yahweh'), abbreviated to J.

Shortly after the death of Solomon (931) appeared another cycle relating to the same events; it dealt with the story of Abraham (Genesis), continuing down to the establishment of the sons of Jacob in the Promised Land in about 1200–1175 (Book of Joshua). This collection is called by biblical scholars the 'Elohist cycle' (abbreviated to E) because in it God is referred to under the name Elohim.

E is written in a far more formal manner than J. It is a studied style, and on that account less stirring than J. It comes from the northern kingdom.

At the time of Hezekiah these two parallel accounts, put down in writing at the end of the tenth century, thus existed side by side. But they had not yet been combined into a single account.

Then, at the time of the fall of Samaria (721), a small body of men of learning succeeded in saving from destruction a summary of the customs of the north and with this precious document they took refuge in Jerusalem. This third version, of great literary beauty, is considered by biblical scholars to be the first elements of the Priestly Code (which was only completed in the fifth century). Its spirit is fundamentally religious. It is known in abbreviation as P.

Thus in the time of Hezekiah in Jerusalem there were in existence three separate traditions which the devout Yahwist was able to read or consult (for at that time writing was fairly widespread in Judah): two accounts

of a popular nature (J and E) and one of priestly in-
spitation (P).

It will be readily understood that this was a national
and historical treasure of a kind unequalled at this period.
Hezekiah was convinced that it was extremely important
to place these works in safety, and no better way could
be found than to combine the three accounts in one
volume. The writers appointed by the king strove their
best to join these accounts together, confining themselves on occasion to setting the various elements side
by side. This explains the contradictions to be found in
some chapters. In the west, since the time of Herodotus, the 'Father of History', the author is expected to
rewrite the narrative, and to unify it, eliminating any
contradictory elements which may occur. In the east, on
the contrary, the writer is unconcerned with contradictions; in an account of the same event he sees
nothing wrong in putting down details which disagree
with those which have been given a few lines previously;
the historian is a mere compiler.

It was not long before the literary team of the *men of
Hezekiah* – to use the biblical expression (Pr. 25:1) – to
whom the king had entrusted this delicate task, noticed
that the story of the national past came to an end at the
time when the Twelve Tribes of Jacob settled in Canaan,
that is, in about 1175. At that time the Chosen People
had just gained possession of the 'Promised Land'
where there *flowed milk and honey*. After the accounts
of these exploits attributed, perhaps, too exclusively to
Joshua, the historian of those days had only short notes
in a fragmentary state for the continuation of the story.
These nevertheless were of undoubted interest for the
period known as that of the Judges, the leaders who
emerged when a group of enemies decided to attack
Israel on its own territory. With the help of this rather sum-

mary information the writers set to work. Using the *Book of the Wars of Yahweh*, a book that no longer exists, the writers took care to rearrange the old national memories of the times of the Judges; but they thought it necessary to bind together the different parts of this composite work with a theological theme. They therefore recopied the ancient narratives in their entirety, and furnished each story with an introduction and a conclusion. This was intended to show beyond any doubt that national misfortunes should be considered as the just punishment of Israel for its infidelity to Yahweh.[7]

Modern biblical scholars of course had no difficulty in distinguishing the change of style between the historical sources, dating from the period of the Judges, and the additions made some four and a half centuries later by Hezekiah's writers.

In the former the language is primitive and archaic with rather rugged images; in the latter the style is elegant, flexible and varied, and shows the signs of a great literary period.

In these circumstances we can reconstruct the genesis of the book of Judges as follows:

At the outset there were separate accounts relating the political and military episodes of a certain tribe or group of tribes.

At the time of Hezekiah the literary men of Judah (a sort of academy) collected these scattered elements together, giving them a uniform theological slant in order

---

[7] In *David* (pp. 4–5), in this series, a description of this four-term equation (a method of explanation suggested by Fr Lagrange) applying to each of these historico-theological pieces was given.

1. Sin: Israel falls into idolatary and worships the Canaanite idols.
2. Punishment: the tribes of Jacob, guilty of idolatry, are made vassals by their Canaanite idols.
3. Sorrow: the Israelites express their repentance to Yahweh.
4. Forgiveness: Yahweh, moved by great mercy, raises up a 'Judge' (a war leader) who will deliver the tribes of Israel from slavery.

Shortly afterwards the same process begins again in another part of the Promised Land.

to transform the separate accounts into one extensive religious lesson (the four-term equation: sin, punishment, repentance, forgiveness).

But at this stage the Book of Judges had still not reached its definitive form. During the following centuries chroniclers completed some of the chapters with incidents which it was considered should be saved from oblivion. The work only reached its final form three centuries later (in about 400 B.C.) at the time of Ezra, that is, on the return from the Babylonian Exile.

For the continuation of the national chronicles after the period of the Judges Hezekiah's Academy had available different accounts which enabled it to lay the foundation of a history of Samuel and David (1040– 970). Following this, for the period of Solomon, Rehoboam and Jeroboam, these historians possessed written information of recent date and of greater accuracy. We no longer possess the narrative drawn up at this time since it was revised and rewritten after the Babylonian captivity.

It should be added that a part of the Book of Proverbs must be credited to the *men of Hezekiah*.[8] In addition, it may be wondered whether at this period these same men of letters had not considerable influence on the writing of one part of the Psalter. This is lyrical poetry in which intimate prayer rises up from the heart; it is addressed to Yahweh in the same way that a man speaks to a powerful protector or even to a friend.

Today a number of biblical scholars think that the literary team working in Jerusalem on behalf of King Hezekiah put into shape the elements of the book which we now call Deuteronomy.

A number of legal sections are scattered about in

---

[8] This is shown by the inscription at the head of *The Second Collection attributed to Solomon* (Pr. 25:1). This reads *The following also are proverbs of Solomon transcribed by Hezekiah, king of Judah*. As has already been explained the ascription to Solomon cannot be taken literally.

Exodus, Numbers, Leviticus among accounts and explanations intended to show us the divine origin of the laws.

The decalogue, the solid foundation of the Law, was promulgated on the slopes of Sinai. With the solemn confirmation of the existence of the one God (already proclaimed five or six hundred years previously to Abraham) there was given the text of a code reduced to a few very short commandments; during the following centuries these were expanded by many explanatory articles, carefully drafted in accordance with the Mosaic tradition.

Clearly God's plan — in addition to the revolutionary declaration about the oneness of God — could not be confined for long to the formulation of a code. Thus as the evolution of the human spirit made it possible, God, speaking through his prophets showed how the law was to be interpreted. This included the love that the faithful follower of Yahweh should give to his Creator, the love that a man should have for his neighbour, the idea of a merciful God to whom a man could lay bare his soul and with whom he could converse with humility and even affection. Thus Deuteronomy effected a deepening of religious awareness, though the Decalogue still remained of course, the basic teaching. In this way the influence of the prophets over Deuteronomy proved decisive.

The 'First Law', promulgated by Moses during the 'forty years' in the wilderness was intended to govern the lives of the shepherds on the plain and was applicable to the conditions of their lives as nomads.

But shortly after the Twelve Tribes had settled in the Promised Land the Mosaic legislation was no longer meeting the needs of the new economic, social or even religious conditions.

Among the Twelve Tribes, and more especially in the kingdom of Samaria an extraordinary development in the Law occurred. To solve the new problems, unknown to the shepherds of the time of Moses, which were arising for the new landowners and citizens of Israel, litigants came to consult the Levites who acted as guardians of the local sanctuaries. They were qualified to give decisions. Thus gradually regional codes were developed, which though always inspired, of course, by the Law of Moses, were adapted to the new conditions. These laws began to be written down on tablets or scrolls and it was thus possible when necessary to refer to them. Of course, these customs of the kingdom of Israel were a reflection of the moral evolution of the period, which was more humane than that of previous times. Thus in the kingdom of Israel, cut off from the sanctuary of Jerusalem by the schism, there originated and developed a new and less severe idea of justice.

In 721 came the fall of Samaria and the destruction of the kingdom of Israel. Some of the Levites, in charge of the sanctuaries of this kingdom took refuge in Jerusalem; they had the presence of mind to bring with them the legislative texts previously written down and these proved a considerable spiritual asset for Judah.

The *men of Hezekiah* lost no time in setting to work on these texts. Their main task was one of classification, followed by that of establishing the indispensible connection between the texts. But the book also has a measured style which shows that the various elements were combined together by someone with impressive literary activities.

This was the procedure, it is probable, adopted by Hezekiah's scribes. In this way was formed the kernel of what at a later period, came to be known as Deuteronomy. Religious customs of the times required that sacred documents of this kind should be deposited near the Ark of the Covenant, in the silence and semi-darkness of the innermost room of the Temple, the Holy of Holies. In the absence of a definite statement it cannot be asserted with certainty that this was done for the precious collection of documents in question. In any case, it would have remained under the care of the priests of the Temple.

The text of Deuteronomy established by Hezekiah's scribes would have been shorter than the book which we can read in our Bible today. Down the centuries the work was progressively embellished by further additions, reflecting fresh social problems with the evolution of civilization; it continued to be augmented with laws and moral principles of an increasingly developed nature.

By our incursion into the golden age of literature at the time of Hezekiah we have been able to realize the richness and spiritual dynamism of this period – end of the eighth, beginning of the seventh century – in which the Hebrew genius shone with incomparable brilliance.

Hezekiah's foreign policy (2 Kings 18–20; 2 Chron. 29–32; Is. 36–39)

In their chronicles the biblical writers deal at length with Hezekiah's foreign policy, though it does not seem very clear in its general plan. Sometimes Hezekiah is shown to us as the faithful vassal of Assyria, and sometimes as the avowed enemy of that country. He appears to be torn between the party in favour of peace, under Isaiah, and the military party with its continual dreams of resuming hostilities against the national enemy. And so we find Hezekiah constantly changing course and taking decisions in formal contradiction with conduct of the day before. In addition, certain episodes do not fit in very well and on occasion the chronology is difficult to determine. There is a general impression of confusion.

Now all this becomes clear if we accept the idea of the King of Judah as a politician playing a double game, from the beginning right up to the end. So long as he feels too weak to throw off the Assyrian yoke he feigns the most complete submission. Then, on several occasions, he believes that he has established a coalition strong enough to raise the standard of rebellion, but he discovers that he has overestimated his strength. Once more he returns to the pacifist fold. These changes of heart are easily explained if we do not lose sight of the fact that he was an ardent patriot – impatient to drive the enemy out of the country. Unfortunately, his unsuccessful attempts to liberate his kingdom obliged him, very unwillingly, to return to the attitude of a contrite and repentant vassal.

Hezekiah's foreign policy can be shown in the form of a drama in five acts.

First Act: 716–705

We must not place excessive trust in the humble and servile attitude which from the time of his accession Hezekiah adopted towards Sargon II, the formidable ruler of Assyria. There was little that the weak king of Judah could hope to attempt against the huge military empire which ruled the Middle East. The only possible policy for Hezekiah was one of collaboration with Assyria. At this time the prophet Isaiah probably warned the young king against any act of open rebellion against Assyria. Any attempt at insurrection would lead to Jerusalem's experiencing at once the fate recently suffered by Samaria. There was no other attitude possible than complete submission to the conqueror.

It would have been very difficult for Hezekiah, therefore, to adopt another policy. As a clever diplomat

**THE ASSYRIAN EMPIRE AT THE TIME
OF ITS GREATEST EXPANSION
UNDER ASHURBANIPAL
(668–621)**

ostensibly he shared the view of the great prophet, the avowed champion of peace.

Yet there can be no doubt that Hezekiah, while revealing it to no one, did not give up his secret desire for revenge. Patiently, he bided his time.

Second Act

In 705 Sargon was murdered in his palace at Khorsabad. Hezekiah thought that the time was ripe, he threw off the mask and rose against Assyria.

Generally speaking, every change of ruler in Assyria was marked by a twofold rebellion. In the capital, groups of ambitious men endeavoured by a coup d'état to seize the crown. At the same time in the vassal countries rebellions broke out in an attempt to be free of the harsh protection of the occupying power.

Sargon, then, had just died. It so happened that on this occasion his son Sennacherib succeeded him without any great difficulty. But already the whole of the Fertile Crescent was in ferment — Babylon, supported by Elam, Tyre and Sidon, refused to pay tribute to Nineveh; that was the usual way of declaring hostilities. In the south of Canaan the Philistines rose. Hezekiah placed himself at the head of a coalition. In the background Egypt fanned the blaze, urging all western Asia to revolt. It seemed as if a general conflagration was imminent.

Isaiah was extremely angry; he tood out against the king and began to predict the great catastrophes that were to engulf the country. Hitherto, Isaiah imagined that he had succeeded in converting the king entirely to his policy. And now, after some ten years of wise government, his royal pupil had broken away. Hezekiah had given up his spiritual guide and gone over openly to the military party. Isaiah's painful surprise is understandable.

Realizing that Sennacherib's advance was the preliminary to an attack on Jerusalem, Hezekiah . . . strengthened his defences: he had the broken parts of the wall repaired . . . 'Sennacherib', said Hezekiah, 'has only an arm of flesh, but we have Yahweh our God to help us fight our battles.' The people took heart at the words of Hezekiah king of Judah.

2 Chronicles 32:2–8

Hezekiah, paying no attention to the prophet's outbursts, continued to carry out his plan. Judaean ambassadors were sent to Egypt to conclude a treaty of alliance and Pharaoh undertook to give military aid. And, as the worst is always to be expected, Hezekiah began to put the defences of Jerusalem in order. The breaches in the ramparts were quickly repaired, new towers were built and a second wall was put up. In view of the importance of water for the city, the king decided to stop up the outlet of the spring Gihon, the principal source of supply, and to make a tunnel, less primitive than the Jebusite Zinnor,[9] to direct the waters of this spring to the interior of the fortifications through a conduit passing beneath the citadel (see Plan, p. 99). A glance at the map of Jerusalem gives an idea of this colossal undertaking. From an inscription discovered on the lining of the tunnel, not far from the entrance, we know that two teams of miners dug towards each other, their tunnel forming a gigantic S (560 yards long). This is the celebrated conduit of Hezekiah, bringing the water from the Gihon spring to the pool of Siloam. To protect this from the enemy Hezekiah enclosed it with a line of fortifications (Hezekiah's wall).

Thus the besiegers when they came would be without water, since the spring of Gihon had been closed on the eastern side, while the besieged would have a plentiful supply.

Despite Isaiah's declarations and forebodings, Hezekiah was sure that the God of Israel would defend the City of David: *'Be strong and stand firm,'* he exhorted his soldiers in a fine speech. *'Be fearless, be undaunted when you face the king of Assyria and the whole horde he brings with him, since he that is with us* (Yahweh)

---

[9] This underground conduit is described in *David* (p. 131–133) in this series.

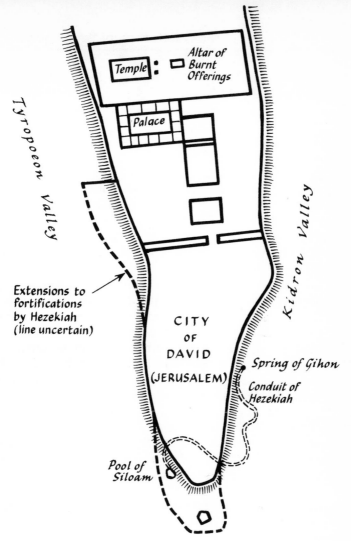

HEZEKIAH'S UNDERGROUND CANAL

The construction of Hezekiah's canal, intended to ensure the water supply to Jerusalem in case of siege, was decided when Sennacherib's armies drew near. Two teams of miners dug towards each other, their tunnel forming a gigantic S, the end of which passed under the city of David. The canal came out on the side of the Tyropoeon Valley in the pool of Siloam under the shelter of the new fortifications constructed by Hezekiah, that is, inside the city. The canal was 560 yards long.

is stronger than he that is with him (the idols of Nineveh)'
(2 Chron. 32:7).

Meanwhile the metal-workers were making *quantities of missiles and shields*.

Hezekiah was already beginning to sing his hymn of victory, while Isaiah was giving vent to his despair, describing the terrible punishment shortly to be experienced by Jerusalem in her pride. For she was placing her trust not in her all powerful God, but in military preparations.

Third Act: Hezekiah's folly, Jerusalem saved by the payment of a heavy tribute

Sennacherib had not yet appeared in Palestine. For three years he was kept in the valleys of the Tigris and the Euphrates where one after another he had to put down serious rebellions. In 701 he had concluded these operations and without delay set out for the land of Canaan.

We can follow his campaign by taking for our guide the baked clay prism of Sennacherib (prism of Taylor), now in the British Museum, in which the king gives the details of his conquests.

Sennacherib's first objective was Phoenicia. Tyre was severely punished and a monarch friendly to Assyria placed on the throne. Sidon fell. The other ports submitted without delay.

Leaving Jerusalem on his left Sennacherib then moved towards Philistia, for he was sure that the Egyptian armies would shortly make their appearance; he would have to cut them in pieces before they could join the coalition. He attacked and captured the strongholds of Ashkelon and Ekron, defended by Philistine garrisons.

Then the Egyptian troops came on the scene. Sennacherib marched to meet them, encountered them at Eltekeh and routed them.

It was now Judah's turn. Hezekiah 'was imprisoned in his capital like a bird in a cage', reads the Assyrian text. Meanwhile, the Assyrian army laid waste the country-side surrounding Jerusalem. 'For my booty,' Senna-cherib informs us, 'I took away men and women, young and old, horses, mules, asses, camels, sheep and cattle in countless numbers.' Soon afterwards the Assyrian cavalry appeared before the walls of Jerusalem and took up its position there; the siege was about to begin.

For Hezekiah the situation was desperate. Obviously he would have done better never to have started on this adventure and would have been wiser to follow the ex-hortations of the Prophet Isaiah who was continually thundering forth:

> *For this day of panic and rout. . . .*
> *They are shouting for help on the mountains.*
> *Elam takes up his quiver,*
> *Aram mounts his horse*
> *And Kir fetches out his shield.*
> *Your fairest valleys*
> *are filled with chariots.* (Is. 22:5–6)

Isaiah saw that this ill-advised adventure must be brought to an end as soon as possible and he advised the king to make an offer of peace without delay. Just then Sennacherib was camped before Lachish whose siege he had just begun. A Judaean embassy was sent to him with a pitiful message from Hezekiah: *I have been at fault. Call off the attack, and I will submit myself to what-ever you impose on me.'* This was surrender pure and simple. Sennacherib did not let the rebel off lightly: as an indemnity he made Hezekiah pay over 300 talents of

---

[10] The mountains: the hills surrounding Jerusalem; Elam and Aram: these non-Assyrian peoples provided the specialist troops — Elam the archers, Aram, the cavalry. Kir, an unidentified country. The chariots were the Chaldaean chariots, the terror of the Judaeans.

silver and 30 talents of gold'[11] *Hezekiah gave him all the silver in The Temple of Yahweh and in the treasury of the royal palace. It was then that Hezekiah stripped the facing from the leaves and jambs of the doors of the Temple of Yahweh . . . and gave it to the king of Assyria* (2 Kings 18:15–16).[12]

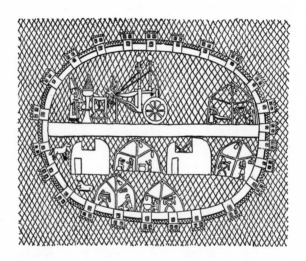

The encampment of Sennacherib before Lachish
The camp was divided into sections. Above, the king's quarters: note his tent, his chariot, and an altar before which two priests wearing special headdresses are officiating. Below, the men's tents, shown in cross-section.
It was a fortified camp, defended by towers which thwarted the possibility of a surprise attack.
After Layard, *Monuments of Nineveh*

Hezekiah was inspired no doubt by a proper patriotism, but also by a very foolish policy which led in the end to a deplorable capitulation that might easily have been avoided if he had listened to the advice of Isaiah, the messenger of peace.

[11] The talent was about 75 lbs.
[12] There has been some discussion about Sennacherib's twofold campaign. Many biblical scholars place the whole thing in 701.

Fourth act: Hezekiah's further imprudent action; Jerusalem providentially saved from destruction

Hezekiah remained impulsive at heart and far too eager to take action; as a consequence he was to experience still further times of difficulty.[13]

In about 690 Hezekiah and Tirhakah fomented a further revolt against Assyria. Sennacherib, informed by his spies, decided to punish his perjured vassal with all severity; he marched on Canaan. First, he laid siege to the southern citadel Lachish, and from there sent his chief cupbearer before the ramparts of Jerusalem whose gates had been closed as a precautionary measure. The population of the city crowded on the walls to hear the important speech which, according to the custom of the times, the besieger's envoy would address to the beleagured city. The Assyrian envoy made a long speech (2 Kings 18:17–37). He said in effect that the Judaeans should not place their trust in Yahweh; in all circumstances the Assyrian gods had shown that they were more powerful than the deities of the vanquished peoples. If Judah agreed to capitulate the inhabitants would be deported to *a land of corn and good wine, a land of bread and of vineyards, a land of oil and of honey* where they would live among plenty. The speaker did not hesitate, it would seem, to show things in the most favourable light. What caused the Judaeans particular distress were the blasphemies uttered against Yahweh, the sarcastic jokes against Yahweh, whose powerlessness, at least from the military point of view, they were bound to admit.

Hezekiah's officials, who had been sent to listen to the message, returned to the king with their garments torn

---

[13] If we adopt the view that Sennacherib conducted two campaigns in succession (701, and then 688), events can be explained as follows: first siege of Jerusalem (701), Assyrian victory; second siege ending with the unexpected withdrawal of the Assyrian troops (2 Kings 19:8).

(a sign of mourning) and reported to him the insults heaped on the God of Israel.

Hezekiah then decided to ask Isaiah's advice. Should he surrender once more and throw himself on the mercy of Sennacherib?

Unexpectedly, Isaiah favoured war, or at least resistance to the Assyrians. *'Yahweh says this,'* he declared. *'Do not be afraid of the words you have heard or the blasphemies the minions of the king of Assyria have uttered against me . . . He will return to his own country!'* (2 Kings 19:6–7).

It was something entirely new to find Isaiah pressing for the continuation of hostilities; hitherto he had urged complete submission to the Assyrian yoke. But directly Sennarcherib began to insult Yahweh the situation was entirely changed, and Isaiah foretold the most terrible misfortunes for the hitherto victorious Assyrian king.

> *Whom have you insulted, whom did you blas-*
> *   pheme?*
> *Against whom raised your voice*
> *and lifted your haughty eyes?*
> *Through your envoys you have insulted the Lord . . .*
>
> *Because you have raved against me*
> *and your insolence has come to my ears,*
> *I will put my ring through your nostrils,*
> *my bit between your lips,*
> *to make you return by the road*
> *on which you came.*[14]   (2 Kings 19: 22, 28)

Fifth act: a miracle – or a providential historical event?

Shortly after the speech by the chief cupbearer before the

[14] The Assyrian bas-reliefs show deported prisoners with a ring through their nostrils and led in a long file like farm animals by the victorious soldiers.

walls of Jerusalem, Sennacherib himself appeared in person, followed by his army. The inhabitants of the city were filled with terror, for they knew how the Assyrians revenged themselves upon those who had broken their word – they could expect plundering, fire and massacre. But Isaiah comforted his fellow-countrymen with these lyrical lines, which he publicly declaimed:

'This then, is what Yahweh says about the king of Assyria'

> *"He will not enter this city,*
> *he will let no arrow fly against it,*
> *confront it with no shield,*
> *throw up no earthwork against it.*
> *By the road that he came on he will return;*
> *he shall not enter this city. It is Yahweh who speaks.*
> *I will protect this city and save it*
> *for my own sake and for the sake of my servant*
> *David"'*   (2 Kings 19:32–34)

In actual fact the Assyrian troops had no time to begin the attack. This is the biblical explanation: *That same night the angel of Yahweh went out and struck down a hundred and eighty-five thousand men in the Assyrian camp.* In the morning the besiegers' tents were filled with corpses. Sennacherib hastened to raise the siege and set out on the way back to his capital on the Tigris.

The biblical writer saw this as an obvious miracle. Isaiah the prophet knew that the holy city would be delivered by an act of Yahweh. The glory of this important event reflected, as was right, both on the prophet and on the God of Israel.

Now an explanation of this event is to be found in Egypt when Sennacherib was obliged to take himself off as quickly as possible. What happened was this. In the fifth century B.C. the Greek historian Herodotus

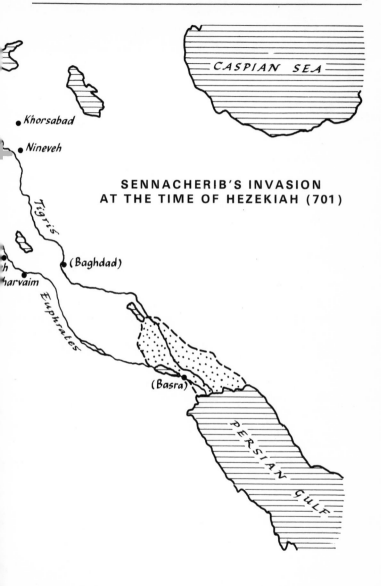

CASPIAN SEA

Khorsabad

Nineveh

**SENNACHERIB'S INVASION
AT THE TIME OF HEZEKIAH (701)**

Tigris

(Baghdad)

harvaim

Euphrates

(Basra)

PERSIAN GULF

heard from the priests of the Valley of the Nile a somewhat similar story in which the hasty departure of the
king of Assyria was related. The Assyrian armies had
just taken up their position before Pelusium, 'at the
entrance to the country', the usual gateway for the
invasion route leading to the Delta. Field rats 'sent by
a god' invaded the tents of the besiegers and devoured
the leather of their quivers, bows and shields. Thus the
besieging army was unable to fight; they could not even
defend themselves and so they were killed in great
numbers. Only a very small number was able to set out
on the return journey (Herodotus II, 141).

According to Herodotus it was therefore a plague
which unexpectedly attacked the Assyrian forces. They
were probably concentrated too closely together in
enormous camps in which, owing to lack of water,
hygienic conditions were of the most primitive kind. In
the ancient east the relationship between swarms of
rats and the incidence of the plague was well established. It is curious to find that both the Egyptian and
Jewish chroniclers should have preserved in scarcely
differing forms the memory of the same scourge. It had
delivered both nations from the grasp of their formidable
common enemy, and both explained the event by divine
intervention.

Sennacherib retired to his own country. The biblical
account continues: *He went into the temple of his god,
and there some of his own children struck him down
with the sword* (2 Chron. 32:21–22). In actual fact the
reign of Sennacherib was to continue prosperously for
a long time. His death only occurred some twenty years
after these events. In any case, after its twofold defeat
before Pelusium and Jerusalem the Assyrian army did
not show its face against in Palestine.

The last years of the reign of Hezekiah do not provide

much material for the historian. Regarding his foreign policy we can conclude that on several occasions he committed gross erros. In the end the city of Jerusalem emerged impoverished indeed, but, materially at least, safe from the ordeal. It must be remembered that the region all around the capital had been transformed into a wilderness. The lesson was a harsh one.

The period of Isaiah

Isaiah had already appeared on the scene at the time of King Ahaz and before that of Hezekiah. We shall encounter him again, quite shortly, in the reign of Manasseh. But quite clearly the period of his decisive action was under Hezekiah. And so a rapid sketch of the moral portrait of this man, who was one of the greatest and most outstanding of the prophets of Israel, falls naturally into place here.

Undoubtedly he was inspired; he has every appearance of the typical prophet, examples of whom we have already encountered in Amos and Hosea. But more than his predecessors he experienced visions and ecstasies. There is the opening scene, for example, in the Temple when he was invested with his office by Yahweh. He hears Yahweh (Is. 5:9; 22:14) with his 'own ears'. Before the gate of the city he proclaims oracles (1:1–6) or laments foretelling future misfortunes (1:21–28). We find him walking naked and barefooted in the streets of the city, predicting the deportations (Is. 20). He performs unusual symbolic actions to predict the tragic events that are to occur. And to gain respect for his prophecies he is not afraid on occasions to state a definite time when his predictions can be verified (Is. 7:16; 29:1).

He is a prophet, of course, but one with unfailing political sense which makes him comparable with a genuine statesman well equipped to guide, in all wisdom and great shrewdness, the diplomacy of the kingdom of Judah. From this point of view, in all the centuries which we have so far examined, the only figure comparable with him is David.

Isaiah's spiritual testament

With so outstanding and rich a personality as Isaiah's we can expect many astonishing revelations. Of all the prophets Isaiah is possibly the one who most of all insisted on the idea of faith as the very condition for the existence of Israel: *'If you do not believe, you will not stand at all'* (Is. 7:9). For the Judaean of the seventh century 'to believe' was to realize that God is present in all circumstances. In this way Yahweh guides the history of the world. So after paying entire homage, after gladly obeying the commandments of the Law, the creature must leave all to the Master of the Universe. That is what was meant by faith.

Another idea dear to Isaiah, and often emphasized by him, was the indestructibility of the Chosen People. An exemplary, well-deserved punishment, of course must be expected — Israel and its capital Samaria had already disappeared, territorially speaking, Judah and Jerusalem were to go in their turn, and at no distant date; but a remnant was to survive, a remnant would return to Yahweh, a small group would be tried by fire to become the keystone of the new spiritual Temple. And that was hope.

On the other hand, as we have seen, on several occasions Isaiah made astounding prophecies about the future when he as it were glimpsed the mysterious figure of 'Immanuel', the divine King, the incarnation of the loftiest virtue. And that was Messianism.

If in a few words we had to state the profound character

of Isaiah's message it could best be done by saying that he came to reveal the 'holiness of God'.

Indeed the first vision which took place in the Temple in Jerusalem shows quite clearly the trend of his later preaching. In this vision seraphs were flying round the central figure of God, singing the triumphal verse:

> *Holy, holy, holy is Yahweh Sabaoth.*
> *His glory fills the whole earth.* (Is. 6:3)

It should be noted that in Semitic languages the adjective 'holy' does not have the meaning of eminent spiritual purity, of the loftiest moral eminence, that we give to it today. The divine Being is 'holy' because he is inaccessible, unapproachable by man. Holiness can therefore be regarded at this period as the synonym of what theologians call 'transcendence' – God's greatness, glory, majesty.

But in the vocabulary of prophecy, then in the full ferment of development, we can perhaps discern the origin of new and dynamic ideas. Increasingly this 'holiness' of God led the believer himself to set himself apart from the profane milieu surrounding him, and, in the next place, from sin which reigned supreme in the groups of primitive peoples.

It is not the least of the glories of Hezekiah's century that it enabled Isaiah to give his message to the world.

II. The long and melancholy reign of Manasseh (687–642)

From 688 (the 'miraculous' liberation of Jerusalem) to 687 was a year, perhaps a year and a half, during which Isaiah and his policy of non-intervention were triumphant. It is quite possible that on his advice Hezekiah resigned himself to the regular payment of his tribute to

Sennacherib; this was a cheap price to pay for the peace which Judah sorely needed.

Manasseh, the new king of Jerusalem

After a reign of twenty-nine years Hezekiah was 'gathered to his fathers'. Unfortunately his son and heir, Manasseh, was then only twelve years old. His mother, who acted as regent, was weak and was obliged to obey Sennacherib's imperious directives (Sennacherib had still six years to live). And indeed it would have been very difficult to oppose the orders of Assyria which just at this period was about to reach the height of its powers.

On attaining his majority Manasseh could only accept the situation imposed on him by force. And throughout his reign he continued to be the Assyrians' faithful vassal. As a result, Judah enjoyed a long period of peace and even, to some extent, of appreciable material prosperity. But now Yahwism could not, as it had done so successfully under Hezekiah, offer a strong enough defence against the evil influences coming both from within the country and from outside influences. In a short space of time it was to be wondered whether, despite the recent reform effected by Isaiah, the Law of Moses would not disappear beneath the irresistible wave of idolatry, supersitition, ancient Semitic beliefs and immoral rites. The situation was the more tragic because Manasseh's reign was to last more than half a century and his influence for a further twenty-five years after his death. Under the suffocating domination of three successive monarchs — Sennacherib, Esarhaddon and Ashurbanipal, who showed no tendency to loosen their merciless grasp, Judah, like most of the other vassal nations, gradually lost her soul.

Yahwism was on its deathbed.

Total decline of religion

The Book of Kings emphasises that Manesseh must be regarded as one of the most wicked kings who ever sat on the throne of David. According to this book of the Bible it appears that from the time of his accession Manasseh adopted a frankly anti-Yahwist attitude and aimed at the methodical destruction of the religion of his fathers. Modern historians do not take so absolute a view. Certain details of the biblical narrative, and our greater knowledge today of the methods adopted by the Assyrians for the assimilation of the conquered nations, enable us to judge Manasseh less severely. Without wishing in any way to lessen his heavy responsibilities, he appears to have been weak. He was lacking in faith, in vigour and also in good fortune. In this way we can account for the development of this tragic decadence.

In those ancient days it was usual for the conqueror to require the vanquished to worship his gods. In the far off centuries when the Canaanites were under the yoke of the Egyptians they were obliged to take part in the solemn worship of Amon and Aton. At the time of Manasseh they were obliged to worship the gods of Niniveh: Ishtar, 'the queen of the sky and of the stars'. They had also to burn incense before the altars set up in honour of the astral deities of the valley of the Tigris, and to celebrate the annual funeral rites of the Babylonian god of vegetation, Tammuz, who died in the autumn and rose again in the spring. In the two courts of Solomon's Temple they worshipped Baal, the powers of Heaven, and the god Shemesh (the sun). Mesopotamian religion had taken possession of the Rock of Jerusalem.

Gradually, as if competing in this return to paganism, the Canaanite rites came back to life. Of course, Manasseh could and ought to have reacted vigorously against this counter-attack of the old idols. Although he did not protect the idolatrous revival officially, he made no law against it; he allowed it to develop freely. And so, on the high places, we find the Baals and idols of Ashtoreth suddenly coming back; everywhere raised stones were put up once more and the sacred poles. In the immediate surroundings of the Temple of Yahweh hostels for the sacred prostitutes of both sexes were established. The ancestral religion of Canaan awakened from its long sleep more threatening than ever.

From Phoenicia, which had preserved the tradition of human sacrifices, especially the sacrifice of young children by burning, these customs returned to the land of Judah. And so we find at this time a revival of this barbarous custom. It was true that despite the vehement prohibitions in Leviticus[15] these customs had never disappeared completely from among the Canaanite groups who made up a large proportion of the population. But in the reign of Manasseh these sacrifices, intended to obtain the deity's favour, assumed proportions hitherto unknown. Manasseh himself sacrificed his own son to Molech, 'the devourer of men'[16] out of mere devotion.

The altars for these vile sacrifices had been put up on mounds of earth in the valley of Ben-Hinnom to the south of the Rock of Jerusalem. There, near the Potsherd gate, these mounds could be seen where the flames from piles of wood burned almost continuously. Devout Yahwists when obliged to pass this place would spit in the direction of the fires as a mark of disgust and reprobation. The place thus came to be known by the name of *tophet* (spittle). Subsequently this site became a place of terror – Gehenna (the valley of Hinnom).

[15] 'You must not pass over any of your children to have them passed to Molech (Moloch) nor must you profane the name of your God in this way. I am Yahweh' (Lev. 18:21).

[16] In reality it was to Baal, who had been given the name of Malek (king), later corrupted into Molech and then Moloch.

It was as if Jerusalem had returned to the times of the Jebusites.

At the same time there occurred a wave of superstitious practices. Conjuring up of the dead had always been practised in Canaan; the Bible describes the frightening scene in the cave of the witch of En-dor where Saul had gone to ask her to put him in touch with Samuel, the dead prophet (1 Sam. 28:3–25). This had happened six hundred years previously.[17] And now Isaiah informs us that in his day, right in the eighth century, these customs were far from being given up in Israel. Sorcery and divination in all their forms also flourished. The king himself supported these 'abominations', as the biblical writer calls them, *and practised soothsaying and magic and introduced necromancers and wizards* (2 Kings 21:6).

It may seem surprising to the reader to find Judah, under its own sovereign in this curious adventure, thus deliberately abandoning its own ancestral God, the one God of the tribes of Jacob. There is however a historical explanation for this.

From the time of Abraham (about 1830) and, even more from the times of Moses (about 1225), Yahweh had progessively revealed himself as the protector of a small group of wandering shepherds of Semitic origin.

First, he was the tribal God of the Twelve Tribes of the descendants of Jacob called Israel. He was the national God at the time of David, who founded the united kingdom of Judah-Israel. Ideas about God were still too obscure, except of course, for a few clear-sighted prophets, for the notion of a universal God to be accepted.

For the time being, therefore, Yahweh, was to remain the only God of the children of Israel *('I am a jealous God')* to whom they had to pay exclusive worship; this was the original character of this new religion. In addition,

[17] See *David* in this series, pp. 101–102.

the Yahwist more or less confusedly admitted the existence of other foreign deities, the protectors of the neigh-
bouring peoples. Nonetheless, in religious circles in
Judah the general conviction was that he was the most
powerful of the gods.

Then, suddenly, and unexpectedly, his power seemed
to wane. Jerusalem became an Assyrian province;
soldiers from the banks of the Tigris were the masters; they
had even installed their idols in Yahweh's own sanctuary.
The people were ashamed and humiliated. And Yahweh
made no move. In the last resort, was the God of Israel
less powerful than the deities imported by the conquerors and set up on the Rock of Zion?

In vain the prophets might proclaim to their contemporaries that the misfortunes of the capital of Judah
were the price exacted for the immorality, perversion
and idolatry engulfing the city of David. No one paid any
attention to these preachers. In the opinion of the ordinary people Yahweh did not come to the help of his
chosen people because he was less powerful than the
gods of their conquerors.

Almost more startling was the fact that Yahweh did
not disappear completely from the religion of Jerusalem;
a place was kept for him in the motley pantheon along
with a number of oriental deities. Thus Yahweh, who
spoke on Sinai, who gave the Decalogue to Moses, was
placed on the same footing as Molech of Tyre, the
Canaanite Baal, the immoral Asherah of Babylon and
the Sun (Shemesh) worshipped at Niniveh.

'Rise, Yahweh, awake!'

There existed in Jerusalem a very small cell of resistance,
determined to carry on. Some of the most heartrending
psalms probably date from this period, particularly the

sorrowful appeal that Jesus was to repeat from the cross:

My God, my God, why have you deserted me?

The inspired writer explains his position; he describes the contempt in which he is held by his fellow-citizens who have gone over to the new gods:

All who see me jeer at me,
they toss their heads and sneer,
'He relied on Yahweh, let Yahweh save him.
If Yahweh is his friend, let Him rescue him!'

Do not stand aside, Yahweh.
O my strength, come quickly to my help;
rescue my soul from the sword,
my dear life from the paw of the dog,
save me from the lion's mouth,
my poor soul from the wild bulls' horns!

(Ps. 22)

The grief of the faithful was the more profound since at this period Yahwist theology, still in a primitive stage, was confined to the exclusive notion of reward or punishment on this earth; any reward after death was for the time being excluded. Such an idea only appeared in Jewish thought towards the end of the Old Testament period (third or second century B.C.).

In any case a small group of Yahwist faithful still lived in hope, deriving from events the lofty moral lesson which had hitherto been unknown to man:

The little the virtuous possesses
outweighs all the wealth of the wicked.

(Ps. 37:16)

Manasseh certainly put an end to the prophetical campaigns which had broken out during the reign of his predecessor Hezekiah. The whole of this opposition party, too turbulent for the new king, was firmly muzzled. The silence of the prophets is sure evidence of this. The voice of Micaiah (Micah) alone was raised from time to time. *Manasseh,* the Second Book of Kings (21:16) tells us, *shed innocent blood, too, in such great quantity that he flooded Jerusalem from end to end.* The metaphor shows that it was a severe persecution. Rabbinical tradition has it that on the occasion of one of these persecutions the prophet Isaiah was sawn in two in a hollow tree. It is not unlikely and is well in tune with the general atmosphere of the period.

A gloomy future for the faithful Yahwist

Although for the time being Yahweh seemed to be unready to act, from one moment to the next his faithful followers expected to see an exemplary punishment, as befitted their blasphemy, fall upon the faithless people. Yahweh's plans were already known and commented on: *'Yaweh, the God of Israel, says this: "Look, I will bring such disaster as to make the ears of all who hear it tingle. I will stretch over Jerusalem the same measuring line as over Samaria . . . I will scour Jerusalem as a man scours a dish and, having scoured it, turns it upside down. I will cast away the remnant of my inheritance,*[18] *delivering them into the power of their enemies, and making them serve as prey and booty to all their enemies, because they have done what is displeasing to me and have provoked my anger" '* (2 Kings 21:13–15). These were hardly comforting predictions.

Amon (642–640): another wicked shepherd of Judah

Amon was as wicked a king as his father. Fortunately he only reigned for two years. He pursued the same policy

[18] The 'remnant': the Judaeans, the only survivors of the Twelve Tribes after the destruction of Samaria.

as his predecessor. Increasingly the official idolatry and sexual cults were flaunted abroad. In the centres of Yahwism (which scarcely deserved the name) there was no concern but for external ritual: the People of God were plunged in thick darkness. The dialogue between Yahweh and his prophet Micah reveals the heart of the matter:

With what gift shall I come into Yahweh's presence
and bow down before the God on high?
Shall I come with holocausts,
with calves one year old?
Will he be pleased with rams by the thousand,
with libations of oil in torrents?
Must I give my first-born for what I have done wrong
the fruit of my body for my own sin?

The answer is clear and forceful:

What is good has been explained to you, man;
this is what Yahweh asks of you:
only this, to act justly,
to love tenderly
and to walk humbly with your God.

(Micah 6:6–8)

The moral law, the heartfelt appeals, proclaimed by the prophets remained a dead letter. Was it then so hard to follow this way? Obviously the flock needed a good shepherd, one worthy of the name, to lead them. With Josiah, the great reforming king, he appeared on the scene.

III. The reign of Josiah, the great reforming king (640–649)

Two years after the death of Manasseh, the zealous servant of the king and gods of Assyria, his grandson,

Josiah, came to the throne. They were two greatly con-trasting characters.

Assyria shows signs of weakness (end of Manasseh's reign)

By about the middle of the seventh century Assyria had succeeded in annexing almost the whole of the ancient east – from the mouths of the Euphrates and the Tigris to the upper valley of the Nile, as far as Thebes, the southern capital of Egypt. The tiny territory of Judah stood thus at the centre of a huge military network, organized on a war footing in which everything was controlled, counted and verified. The Assyrian power seemed built on foundations of granite.

In actual fact it was a colossus with feet of clay. The empire was too vast. Of course, it dominated all its vassal states by fear, and its armies were continually on the march from one end to the other of the Fertile Crescent to suppress rebellions in baths of blood. But a system of government like this could not hold together for long. It was bound, in a relatively short time, to fall to pieces.

At the time when Manasseh was coming to the final years of his reign Ashurbanipal, the ruler of Assyria, had pushed the frontiers of his empire further than any of his predecessors. But in less than a century, as we shall see, there occurred the rapid and complete collapse of his empire.

A few chronological details will enable us to follow the course of this drama.

652: A general revolt in Babylon, Elam, Syria and also, probably, in Judah.[19]

[19] It is at this point, in my view, that the (temporary and very short) 'captivity' of Manasseh in Babylon should be placed. It is very probable that this poor king, hitherto obliged to obey his overlord Ashurbanipal, thought it opportune to join the general plot against Assyria: *Then Yahweh sent the generals of the king of Assyria against them, who captured Manasseh with hooks* (rings through the nose or lips), *put him in chains* (fetters which nevertheless allowed him to

665. The Assyrian forces occupying the Nile corridor were thrown out of Egypt by Pharaoh Psammetichus I (663–609) who declared his independence. At the same moment a European invasion occurred. The Medes came from southern Russia through the Caucasus and began to threaten the valley of the Tigris to the south of the Caspian Sea. The future looked sombre for Assyria.

There were other alarms: the nomads of the Syrian wilderness took advantage of the weakness of Assyria to carry out raids on Edom, Moab and Transjordania.

Not without difficulty Ashurbanipal finally succeeded in overcoming these rebels; but he did not feel himself strong enough to try to reconquer Egypt, which was able to preserve its somewhat aggressive independence. It seems that in these circumstances, in return, no doubt, for a renewed oath of allegiance, Ashurbanipal decided to restore Manasseh to freedom and to his throne in Jerusalem; Judah had then to act as a buffer state facing the Egyptian frontier.

All this activity is clear evidence of the irrespressible aspirations of the countries of the east as they tried to recover their freedom. These events took place between 665 and 648, and it was precisely in 648, it is worth emphasizing, that Josiah was born.

---

walk) *and led him away to Babylon* (2 Chron. 33:11). A short time ago this story was regarded as a picturesque invention of the chronicler's. Today, when we are better acquainted with the events of the ancient east, as a result of the discovery of Assyrian documents, the incident in which Manasseh figures fits perfectly with the historical context of the period. Indeed the precise statement 'to Babylon', which seemed to be a clear blunder (Nineveh seemed the more likely place), is fully confirmed by the fact that at this period (653) Ashurbanipal had just put down a rebellion in the neighbourhood of Babylon; he had then seized this great city and was staying there temporarily.

Probably Manasseh succeeded in clearing himself. He was sent back to Jerusalem and his crown was then returned to him.

The Bible tells us that in the last years of his reign Manasseh repented of his apostasy and removed from the Temple the altars and idols of the foreign gods which had previously been introduced there. It was a very tardy gesture with scarcely any influence over the widespread idolatry among the people. More-over, Amon, Manasseh's son and the father of Josiah, on his own account continued the campaign in favour of the foreign gods.

The four principal divisions of the reign of Josiah (640–609)

Manasseh died in 642. His son Amon reigned scarcely two years.

640: Josiah, the heir to the throne was proclaimed king. He was a child of eight.

For a better understanding of this important reign it will be here divided into four principal periods:

The regency (640–632).

The awakening of the young king's Yahwist conscience (632–630) which coincides (significantly) with a series of severe Assyrian defeats.

Josiah's great religious reform (630–621) under the guidance of Jeremiah.

Finally, in 621, the 'discovery of the Book of the Law'.

Precisely at this moment the death of Ashurbanipal occurred and the rapid decline of Assyria began; and from 621 to 609 work on the Priestly Code was begun; its definitive composition was to take place in the following two centuries B.C.

Eight years of regency

Once more there was government by queen mother. On this occasion, fortunately, the blunders which marked the beginning of the reign of Manasseh were avoided. It was true that the international situation was quite different. Jerusalem no longer felt quite so suffocated as formerly under the harsh Assyrian overlordship. From the beginning of the first half of the seventh century Assyria was obliged by force of circumstances to slacken its hold and life was easier in Jerusalem. And so the young king's tutors, carefully chosen by the Royal Council, took care that he should receive a completely orthodox religious education. Although on this point the biblical writers give little information, the king's behaviour during his thirty-year reign leaves no doubt about the solid principles of Yahwism that he was taught from an early age.

For the time being in Judah there could be no question of undertaking thoroughgoing reforms. Ashurbanipal still remained the master, in name at any rate. And the Temple of Yahweh, dominating the city of David, was still defiled by the presence of the Assyrian deities and the sacred prostitutes.

But there was one change, though hardly a spectacular one, which was rich in promise for the future. Within the privacy of the palace priests were educating the young king in respect for true morality, for justice and for that spiritual religion which is the distinctive mark of Yahwism.

The awakening of the Yahwist conscience of the young king (632–630); The Scythians, the prophet Zephaniah

632: Josiah was sixteen.

At about this time hordes of Scythian horsemen (Indo-Europeans who came in the wake of the Medes) burst through the north-east bastion of the Assyrian defences and for ten years overran the territories of Mesopotamia and Canaan.[20] They even arrived at the Egyptian frontier. Psammetichus managed to turn them back by payment of a large tribute.

The proud and powerful Assyrian Empire had suffered a heavy blow. Ashurbanipal never succeeded in halting this wave of barbarians who for years overran his possessions from one end to the other, plundering and laying waste the countryside, burning the villages and

[20] According to Herodotus the Scythian invasion ravaged the Middle East for twenty-eight years. Today the tendency is to reduce this to ten years or less 632–622). During this period a great number of Scythians were absorbed into the native populations; after this raid the remainder of these bands returned to their country of origin.

sowing destruction and misery everywhere. The prestige of Assyria was seriously impaired. The knell had sounded for Assyrian power.

It was just at this time in Jerusalem that the prophet Zephaniah could be heard thundering against the Assyrian domination which had dared to introduce its vile gods into the House of Yahweh. Zephaniah foretold the approaching collapse of the nation which half a century previously had cut the territory of Judah in half. But Yahweh was making ready, the prophet asserted, to bring to nothing this foreign power, the embodiment of evil, which for this reason had provoked hate on all sides.

> *He is going to raise his hand against the north*
> *and bring Assyria down in ruins;*
> *He will make Nineveh a waste,*
> *dry as the desert.*
> *In the middle of her flocks will rest*
> *all the beasts of the valley,*
> *even the pelican and the heron*
> *will roost round her cornices at night;*
> *the owl will hoot at the window*
> *and the raven croak on the doorstep . . .*
>
> *Is this the joyful city,*
> *so confident on her throne,*
> *who said in her heart,*
> *'Here am I, with none to equal me'?*
> *What a ruin she is now,*
> *a lair for beasts!*
> *All those who pass by her*
> *whistle and shake their fists.* (Zeph. 2:13–15)

After the punishment which was to fall on the hated nation, the prophet foretold for Judah a wonderful national restoration based on religious reform.

The young king grew up in this curious atmosphere which encouraged all kinds of hopes. At last Assyria was to collapse. Could there be any doubt of it?

Josiah's first reforms: the Temple cleansed and restored to Yahweh

In 628 the king was twenty. It is quite probable that this year saw his first great reform for the cleansing of the Temple: this was the removal of the idols (doubly hateful because in addition to their religious significance they had also a political one), abolition of the offensive cults established in different parts of the sanctuary, and the return of the Temple to Yahweh and his servants.

It is clear that Josiah was following in the footsteps of his great-grandfather Hezekiah; he was very like him in many ways, particularly by his overriding vocation as a reformer. These two kings stand out as convinced Yahwists and men of action determined to adopt measures which would guide the People of God back to the straight path. All the same, it should be emphasized that Josiah emerges as far greater and nobler than his ancestor.

Like Hezekiah in his day, Josiah decided to throw the Assyrian deities out of the Temple where they had once more taken possession. The high priest Hilkiah, his subordinates and the 'guardians of the threshold' received orders to throw out of the sanctuary all the cult objects made for Baal and the *whole array of heaven* (this referred to the astral cult, a favourite in Mesopotamian religions). These objects were taken to the fields of Kidron and burned. The king ordered the houses of the sacred prostitutes established within the Temple precincts, near the place where women wove the garments for Asherah, to be pulled down. The priests who had offered sacrifices to Baal, to the Sun and Moon were to be deprived of their offices.

In the lesser buildings of the sanctuary the chariot of the Sun was kept together with the sacred horses during the ceremonies organized in honour of the gods of the zodiac. Josiah slaughtered the horses and burned the chariots.

On the terrace of the Temple previous kings of Judah had built small altars in honour of the gods of the sky. Manasseh had also put up sacrificial altars in the two Temple courts. All these 'abominations' were pulled down and the rubble flung into the Kidron valley.

The city of Jerusalem itself and the immediate neighbourhood had to be purified in their turn.

At the gate of Joshua (called after a governor of the city) stood the shrine of the goats (probably demons with the appearance of satyrs); it was pulled down.

It was also necessary to destroy as soon as possible the loathsome Tophet, the furnace where impious Israelites continued to burn their new born as sacrificial victims for Molech. Josiah desecrated this place by establishing on its site the refuse dump for the city.

On the other side of the Kidron, on the western slope of the Mount of Olives there stood the religious buildings put up by Solomon for his pagan wives; there was a temple for Ashtoreth of the Sidonians, another for Shemesh of the Moabites and for Milcom of the Ammonites. All these were pulled down.

To desecrate the altars of the foreign gods the bones of their former priests were burned on them. Then the sacrificial objects were destroyed; the stone statues were hammered to pieces, the bronze effigies were broken up and the fragments scattered on the tombs of those who had formerly taken part in these loathsome rites.

The same methods were adopted on the 'high places' situated at the summits of the wooded hills where the primitive Canaanites worshipped their gods. After the conquest of the Promised Land the Yahwists had indeed organized ceremonies for the worship of Yahweh in these same places but usually had kept the statues of the old gods. This was nothing else than a shameful syncretism in which Yahweh was invoked at the same time as the sexual deities.

Josiah and the priests of Jerusalem intended to abolish for ever these curious shrines which were an insult to orthodox theology. One after the other systematic measures of desecration and destruction were applied to them. The steles were thrown down, the sacred poles sawn up. Human bones were scattered on the ground to desecrate these sites.

Josiah did not confine his activities to the territory of Judah; the increasing relaxation of Assyrian vigilance enabled him to extend his campaign of religious restoration to the former kingdom of Samaria. His envoys traversed the cities belonging to the tribes of Manasseh, Naphtali and Simeon, where there were still a few small pockets of Israelites. The religious reformers then carried out a thoroughgoing destruction on the high places. The biblical writer even tells us that the priests of these shrines were sacrificed on their own altars.

The priests of the high places of Judah were treated more humanely. After the destruction of their local shrines, they were summoned to Jerusalem and concentrated round the Temple. It was thought, probably, that it would be dangerous to leave centres of resistance in existence in the remote regions of the country. It was preferable to have these men in Jerusalem. Their board and lodging was provided at the expense of the religious community. But they were not given the privilege of serving in the Temple nor, of course, of taking part in the sacred rites.

The restoration of authentic Yahwist worship, rid at

last of the Assyrian, Canaanite and other rites, was obviously the aim of the circle of prophets centred on Jerusalem.

But Josiah, who was the devoted servant of this religion now restored to its ancient purity, had another, national aim in view. The centralization of worship in Jerusalem implied centralization of the government of Judah-Israel, now practically restored. Very shortly, the City of David would become once more, it could be hoped, the sole capital of the land occupied by the People of God. At this time the prophet Zephaniah was joyfully announcing the coming deliverance, the return to social peace and unity restored at last:

> *Shout for joy, daughter of Zion,*
> *Israel, shout aloud! . . .*
> *Yahweh your God is in your midst,*
> *a victorious warrior.*
> *He will exult with joy over you,*
> *he will renew you by his love;*
> *he will dance with shouts of joy for you*
> *as on a day of festival.*   (Zeph. 3:14–17)

The biblical writers, both of the second Book of Kings and of Chronicles, are full of admiration for Josiah's reforms. *He did what is pleasing to Yahweh, and in every respect followed the example of his ancestor David, not deviating from it right or left* (2 Kings 22:2; 2 Chron. 34:2).

Even if the task of purification had gone no further, Josiah would have deserved praises of his historians, but after an entirely unexpected occurrence, the movement for renewal was to take on a new form and new life.

The finding of the Temple of the Book of the Law
(2 Kings 22:3–10; 2 Chron. 34:11–18)

With picturesque details the Bible tells the story of this discovery which took place in the eighteenth year of the reign of Josiah (621). He was then just twenty-five.

Masons and carpenters under the direction of the Levites were then at work repairing the Temple. Now, as the high priest Hilkiah was collecting the silver brought by the faithful for the restoration of the temple he found – the writer gives no further detail – an old document which he had scarcely any difficulty in identifying directly he unrolled it. *'I have found the Book of the Law.'* he told Shaphan, the secretary. Shaphan hurried to the king and read the work to him. As the reading progressed the king became increasingly worried; with terror in his heart he heard the curses threatening those who transgressed these commandments. *'Great indeed must be the anger of Yahweh,'* he explained to his entourage, *'blazing out against us because our ancestors did not obey what this book says by practising everything written in it.'* And as a token of his shame and sorrow he *tore his garments*.

Before taking an official decision Josiah had to be certain of the authenticity of the document. He asked the advice of Huldah, a 'prophetess' who lived in the new city. Huldah declared that the manuscript contained the words of Yahweh, and she added, *'The anger of Yahweh is blazing out against this people'*.

Terrified, and with reason, Josiah summoned the elders, and the men of Judah and Jerusalem; in their company, and escorted by priests and Levites, he went up to the Temple. There, before the assembled company he read out aloud *everything that was said in the book of the covenant found in the Temple of Yahweh*. Standing beside one of the two pillars at the entrance, he solemnly promised on his own behalf and on that of his subjects to keep the commandments, the decrees and laws which had just been revealed to them; and he promised Yahweh to *enforce the terms of the covenant as written in that book*. Thus Judah was consecrated to Yahweh anew in an imposing ceremony like that held by Moses on Sinai and also by Joshua at the entrance of the Chosen People into the Promised Land.

Even before the discover of the Law Josiah (as we have seen, following the account in Chronicles), had carried out a thoroughgoing reform relying on oral traditions and following the counsels of the prophets or asking the advice of Yahwists reputed for their piety or wisdom. In future, with this document so providentially discovered the king and lawgiver was in a position to take his stand on a definite text, on a written law.

This code, in the hands of a king who was already determined to reform the civil and religious institutions of his country, was to be the cause of a powerful and original movement of legislation; and also, it was to be hoped, of a moral revolution which was greatly needed in Judah.

Critical examination of this discovery of the Book of the Law

Was this Book of the Law really 'discovered' in the Temple as reported by the biblical writer?

For the representative of the school of higher criticism of the end of the last century the explanation was very simple: the code was a fraudulent fabrication from beginning to end by the priests of Jerusalem. Then, with or without the king's consent, they pretended to discover it so that it could be used as the justification for further reforms.

There is another and more acceptable explanation.

It is now known that in those ancient days documents of exceptional importance were often placed in sanctuaries in hiding-places known to a few priests only. Years passed, and the memory of these secret hiding-places was often lost. Many centuries later, when no one even remembered their existence, the documents were discovered. This sort of thing could be matched in the Middle Ages both in Europe and in Islam. Thus in Jerusalem, when one of the pillars of the El Aqsa mosque was being repaired (it stands on the Temple esplanade) a twelfth-century Latin letter was discovered in 1926; it was written by Gerard de Ridefort, the Seneschal of the Templars.

Perhaps it is not necessary, therefore, to explain the discovery of the Book of the Law as a pious fraud, as the higher critics ingenuously suggest, despite the lack of information about certain religious customs of the ancient east. There seems no real reason why we should not accept the biblical account of the event.

The origin of Deuteronomy

The origin of the Book which was one day to be called Deuteronomy can be accounted for in this way.

First stage. We have seen how in 721 Levites of the kingdom of Samaria, fleeing from Assyrian suppression, took refuge in Jerualem. They brought with them local codes in which were preserved in writing the laws and customs of the northern kingdom.

Second stage. In about 700 in Jerusalem 'the men of Hezekiah' gathered these various codes together into a single body of law. It was a fairly thin scroll and formed the nucleus of what at a later date was to be called the Second Law. The text in question must certainly have been recopied, but the number of copies can only have been restricted. Religious custom required that one of these copies should be deposited in the Temple so that it could be referred to on occasion.

Third stage. In the time of Manasseh, when orthodox Yahwists suffered a long and harsh persecution, it is probable that this original copy could no longer continue to occupy a place of honour in the sanctuary; it was therefore relegated to some quite ordinary place unless a group of priests, faithful to the Law of Moses, took the precaution of hiding it.

Fourth stage. In 621 during the work for the restoration of the Temple and its dependencies a document dating back about a hundred years was discovered; the high priest Hilkiah found no difficulty in recognizing the Book of the Torah or Book of the Covenant.[21]

In previous references the chronicler called it *the book of the Law given through Moses* (2 Chron. 34:14).[22] Following the example of several Fathers of the Church (Saints Jerome, Athanasius, John Chyrsostom among others) a group of modern biblical scholars believe that the document discovered in 621 was merely a copy of the code of Hezekiah which had fortunately escaped the systematic destruction carried out under Manasseh. The text was relatively short for there were two successive readings of it, one by Hilkiah, the second, aloud, by Shaphan in the king's presence (2 Chron. 33:15, 18; 2 Kings 22:8, 10).

Fifth stage (621–609). Directly after the discovery of the Book of the Law messengers were sent by Josiah to all the regions of Judah and also to the shrines of the

[21] The fact that Hilkiah recognized the 'Law of Yahweh' at first sight shows that it had survived, at least in part, in oral form during the reign of Manasseh; the prodigious memories of easterners is well known and their faculty of preserving lengthy narratives in this way for several generations. The new factor here was this: there was now a complete and not a fragmentary document in existence, and one that left no room for argument.

[22] Several modern authors take the view that the scroll found by Hilkiah referred to the Mosaic Covenant (the Law given on Sinai) whose spirit was obscured by the Covenant of David, in force in Jerusalem for some centuries past.

former kingdom of Samaria. With full authority they informed the followers of Yahweh of the new laws to be observed in future. It is very probable that to help them in their work these travelling preachers made several copies of the book in this version and that this, in accordance with the custom of the times was soon embellished with glosses (marginal explanations) of local laws discovered in some places.

Last stage. This primitive form of Deuteronomy, originating in the time of Hezekiah, forgotten in the reign of Manasseh, enlarged under Josiah, did not assume its definitive form until the period of the exile: it then became, together with the Priestly Code, the keystone of Judaism at a time when the prophetic influence was progressively declining.

Unexpected failure of Josiah's reform

The biblical writers give us scarcely any information of importance about the period of twelve years from the discovery of the Book of the Law (621) to the death of Josiah on the battlefield at Megiddo (609). They refer us to 'The Book of the Annals of the Kings of Judah' (2 Kings 23:28) or to 'The Book of the Kings of Israel and Judah' (2 Chron. 35:27). Neither of these books has survived.

They inform us however of the important religious reorganization of the priesthood. At the Passover which followed the first reading of the Law a great festival took place: *No passover like this one had ever been celebrated in Israel since the days of the prophet Samuel*, the chronicler notes with admiration. From that day onward, and following the prescriptions laid down in the Book of the Law, Jacob's descendants were to be scrupulous in their observance of the Passover and, for seven days, the feast of unleavened bread.

133

With what we know of the fine reform effected by Josiah we might expect to notice a profound spiritual transformation taking place in the nation. But this did not occur.

At the beginning of this religious campaign the prophet Jeremiah was loud in his enthusiasm. He was full of hope for the return of Judah to its tutelary deity. In addition, when the new Law had to be proclaimed to the people of the cities and the countryside, it appears that Jeremiah took his place among the fervent missionaries who were to preach it.[23]

But soon the prophet noticed that this reform had effected very little change in the soul of the Judaeans and Israelites. They confined themselves generally to observance of the external forms, especially the centralization of worship in Jerusalem. And without even trying to reform themselves morally they imagined that their relations with Yahweh were perfect.

According to Jeremiah, the people ought not to have confined themselves to this outward transformation. In the religion of Yahweh what was principally important was to practice obedience to the Law of Moses, that is, spiritual fidelity. And so we find the forceful images in the 'oracle of Yahweh' proclaimed by Jeremiah in the name of God.

Circumcise yourselves for Yahweh,
Off with the foreskin of your hearts. (Jer. 4:4)
Plainly their ears are uncircumcised. (Jer. 6:10)
The whole House of Israel is uncircumcised at heart. (Jer. 9:25)

Conversion to Yahweh meant 'circumcision of the heart', that is, the religious life of the soul. All the rest was

[23] *Proclaim all this in the towns of Judah and in the streets of Jerusalem: 'Listen to the words of this covenant and obey them'* (Jer. 11:6).

hypocrisy. At a later date St Paul was to return to this image: real circumcision, what marks God's faithful servant, is circumcision of the heart.

Quite obviously the Judaeans were a long way from so lofty a moral standard: *'Judah, her* (Israel's) *faithless sister, has not come back to me in sincerity, but only in pretence – it is Yahweh who speaks'* (Jer. 3:10).

And so Jeremiah began to proclaim publicly the terrible catastrophe which was shortly to befall the unfaithful city:

> *'. . . my wrath* (will) *leap out like a fire,*
> *and burn with no one to quench it,*
> *in return for the wickedness of your deeds.'*
>
> (Jer 4:4)

As a matter of fact very shortly we shall see this anger fall on the optimistic and self-satisfied people who, with the help of a few ritual observances, believed that they were under the protection of their God.

Thus despite his good will and his courage, Josiah did not succeed in bringing back the Chosen People to the path of their traditional religion.

612 – the destruction of Nineveh

The destruction of Jerusalem took place in 587. But twenty-six years previously there occurred the destruction of Nineveh, the capital of the immense Assyrian Empire.

To modern readers of the Bible this may appear a mere episode of ancient history. But to contemporaries of the event the fall of this city marked the end of a fearful nightmare. At the slightest sign of unrest the vassal states could expect the merciless Assyrian armies to descend upon them. Their methods of repression were well known: they turned the countryside into a wilderness,

tearing down and burning cities, decimating the population, and carrying off to remote countries the survivors
of the slaughter. 'Over the smoking ruins,' relates one of
these monarchs on one of the inscriptions of his palace,
'my face lights up; in the assuaging of my anger I find my
pleasure.' The explosion of joy which shook the whole
of the Middle East at the news of this liberation can well
be imagined. The face of the Middle East was completely
changed.

It was a city of incredible, legendary wealth. Nineveh
should be regarded as the combination of several great
cities, each with their own fortifications, citadel, palaces
and temples. At about twelve miles from Nineveh stood
Dur Sharrukin (Sargontown, it might be called, since
Sargon, its founder, desired to give it his name; today it is
Khorsabad). It was defended by an enclosure nearly
four miles in circumfrence. Nineveh itself was surrounded
by a wall nine miles long. Twenty-one miles to the south
of the capital was Calah (today Nimrud) where Assurna-
sirpal II, Shalmaneser III, Tiglath-Pileser III and Esarhaddon had their palaces, bursting with booty, the spoil
from the vanquished nations. Between these immense
cities stretched an almost uninterrupted line of small
places; *tels* or hillocks, mark the site of their ruins. By
their suburbs and gardens all these urban centres were
almost joined together

This huge conglomeration stood within an enclosure
some fifty-six miles long. In short, the whole thing seemed
like an enormous entrenched camp surrounded by
fortified towns.[24]

Nineveh (Ninua in Assyrian), situated at the heart of
this extraordinary urban complex, was a city built on two
hills, transformed into citadels which dominated the

[24] A. Brou, *Histoire ancienne des peuples de l'Orient* (pp. 201–3); Maspero,
Histoire ancienne de l'Orient classique (pp. 466–71).

river on the left bank. The Tigris was confined by brick and stone quays, built by Sennacherib. He it was also who put up formidable defences on the opposite bank calculated to discourage the hardiest of attackers. A wall three miles long surrounded the city with a ditch behind it; then there were two demi-lunes and finally a double rampart for two and a half miles. Within this great city Sennacherib dwelt in a palace which covered nearly five acres; it was defended by battlemented walls and fortified towers. The royal dwelling was built with beams of sandlewood and cedar, adorned with inlays of ivory. The inside walls were covered with bas-reliefs and inscriptions recounting the sovereign's mighty deeds. Close at hand stood another palace, a marble one this time, in which the treasure was kept. Kings Esarhaddon and Ashurbanipal also lived at Nineveh. Ashurbanipal founded a library there unique for its period. The British archaeologist Layard discovered on its site thousands of clay bricks, copied from ancient Babylonian examples classified and catalogued.

How did this city, regarded as impregnable, fall into the hands of the new Babylonian dynasty in alliance with the Indo-European Medes who had just appeared in this corner of Asia?

Shortly before 612 Nahum the prophet described the collapse of the proud city:

> 'Woe to the city soaked in blood,
> full of lies,
> stuffed with booty,
> whose plunderings know no end.
>
> I (Yahweh) mean to lift your skirts as high as your face
> and show your nakedness to nations,
> your shame to kingdoms.

*I am going to pelt you with filth,
shame you, make you a public show.'*
(Nah. 3:1, 5–6)

The following was the course of events.

A few years previously Cyaxares, king of the Medes, had tried to seize Nineveh. Attracted by the enormous riches piled up in the city he had laid siege to it. But the Assyrians saved their city with the help of Scythian mercenaries, intrepid horsemen and, incidentally, kinsmen of the Medes.

But this was only a postponement of the evil day. Cyaxares, who was methodical in his plans of conquest, soon returned to the attack; we have evidence of this in the prism of Nabonidus discovered by Fr Scheil. On this occasion Cyaxares formed an alliance with Nebupolassar, the founder of the neo-Babylonian dynasty, which was to play a decisive part in Asiatic affairs and more especially in the Judaean tragedy which was to occur very soon.

Nebupolassar was an ambitious, energetic soldier, probably of Chaldaean origin, who took advantage of the weakness of Ashurbanipal, his sovereign, to seize the city of Babylon and the country of the same name (616). In 615 the new sovereign of Babylon concluded with Cyaxares the military alliance mentioned above. The two warriors, joining forces, laid siege to Nineveh, which fell to them after a long siege in the month of *Ab* (July–August) 612. According to the historian Abydenus, Sarakos, king of the Assyrians, burnt himself alive in his palace together with his wives and children rather than fall into the hands of the besiegers.

The metropolis of the Middle East was destroyed for ever. An empire which for centuries had terrorized the Middle East disappeared entirely.

A handful of soldiers under the command of Ashur-uballit II, the last king, managed to take refuge in the upper valley of the Euphrates at Haran, a fortified city, where they held out for some time.

Nineveh itself, sacked and burnt to the ground, fell into oblivion almost at once. Soon even the site on which it stood was forgotten. Two centuries later the Greek captain Xenophon, at the head of his celebrated body of 'ten thousand', then in retreat, passed near the ruined capital without even suspecting its presence.

'Once Nineveh had fallen Assyria no longer existed,' writes Maspero. In its general sense the remark is true. Nevertheless the death throes of Assyrian power lasted for six years more, long enough to cause Judah the worst misfortunes.

Josiah's death on the battlefield of Megiddo (609)

After the fall of Nineveh the two conquerors shared the empire between them: Cyaxares took Assyria itself and its dependencies in the upper valley of the Tigris, as well as the regions, still in a very barbarous state, situated to the north and the east; Nebupolassar, who had proclaimed himself king of Babylon twelve years previously, became the overlord of the lower plain of Elam, the Mesopotamian regions of the banks of the Euphrates, Syria and the land of Canaan.

At Haran, as has been mentioned, was the last remnant of the Assyrian forces.

This is the historical context in which the Judaean catastrophe occurred, with the death of Josiah on the battlefield of Megiddo.

Ever since ancient times Canaan had been the cockpit between Egypt and the powers of the north (whether they were Hittite, Assyrians or Babylonians). By definition the Egyptians regarded as a national enemy any sovereign to the north of the source of the Jordan who appeared to have intentions of seizing, annexing or laying under tribute the territory which we now call Palestine.

For this reason it is surprising to find Neco II, the son of Psammetichus, concerned about the misfortunes of the Assyrians and going to the aid of their king. Of course, a very weak or powerless Assyria suited Neco admirably, but as a clever diplomat it did not fit in his plans at all for his hereditary rival to be replaced on the Mesopotamian chessboard by the neo-Babylonian empire. Its sovereign, Nebupolassar, made no secret of his plans for hegemony. This is the explanation of the unexpected aid that Neco wanted to give to his hereditary enemy.

To reach the Euphrates Neco had to cross the land of Canaan from one end to the other.

It was against the traditional policy of Judah to allow a foreign army to cross its territory. Neco's request, framed in courteous terms, was refused, and Josiah crossed the mountains of Samaria and made his way at the head of his weak forces to the gap of Megiddo, a strategic point on the plain of Jezreel where many decisive battles had been fought in past ages. It was madness for this petty king to think of opposing the powerful Egyptian army. The Judaeans were cut in pieces. During the battle Josiah was mortally wounded; he was then only thirty-nine (609).

The king's body was taken back to Jerusalem. *All Judah and Jerusalem mourned for Josiah*. The ritual lamentations were chanted. The people of God might well observe a period of national mourning: twenty-three years exactly after the death of Josiah the reformer, not one stone remained upon another in the city of David.

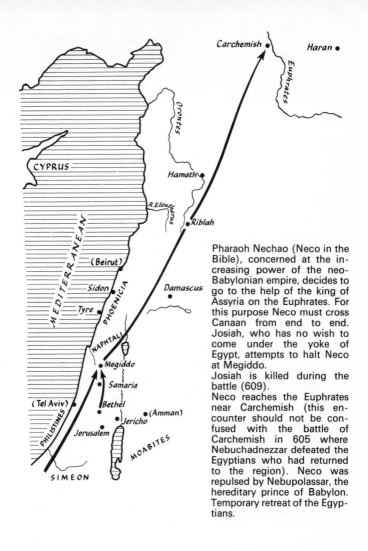

Pharaoh Nechao (Neco in the Bible), concerned at the increasing power of the neo-Babylonian empire, decides to go to the help of the king of Assyria on the Euphrates. For this purpose Neco must cross Canaan from end to end. Josiah, who has no wish to come under the yoke of Egypt, attempts to halt Neco at Megiddo.

Josiah is killed during the battle (609).

Neco reaches the Euphrates near Carchemish (this encounter should not be confused with the battle of Carchemish in 605 where Nebuchadnezzar defeated the Egyptians who had returned to the region). Neco was repulsed by Nebupolassar, the hereditary prince of Babylon. Temporary retreat of the Egyptians.

PHARAOH NECO GOES TO FIGHT THE NEO-BABYLONIAN POWER ON THE BANKS OF THE EUPHRATES
DEATH OF JOSIAH DURING THE BATTLE OF MEGIDDO (609)

IV. The disastrous reign of Jehoiakim: the beginning of the end (609–589)

The vigorous reforms set on foot by Josiah gave grounds for hope of a spiritual recovery in Judah, if only the effort were continued by his successors. But the four kings who were to succeed him on the throne of David[25] commited so many blunders in their domestic and foreign policy that twenty years after the death of Josiah the kingdom of Judah collapsed. And so we see the plundering and burning of Jerusalem, the destruction of the Temple of Yahweh and, finally, the deportation of the leading citizens from Judah to Babylon.

Jehoiakim's disastrous reign, which began the series of catastrophes, falls logically into three distinct parts: Judah, the vassal of Pharaoh Neco II (609–606); Judah, the vassal of the Babylonian king Nebuchadnezzar (606–602), rebels against its overlord, thus provoking an immediate and terrifying reaction by the Babylonian power (602–598); and just at the time when Jehoiakim died Nebuchadnezzar's armies appeared before the walls of Jerusalem. The end of the city was near.

Jehoiakim, vassal of Pharaoh Neco II (609–606)

After disdainfully pushing aside the tiny Judaean army at Megiddo where Josiah met his death, Neco continued his way towards the Euphrates where he expected to match his strength against the forces of Nebupolassar, the king of Babylon.

It was a drawn battle, fought by the banks of the great river. Neco was determined to continue the battle at the first opportunity, but for the time being retired a short

[25] There were four of them, though only two are important historically. The chronological list is as follows:
1. Jehoahaz, son of Josiah; reigned three months in 609.
2. Jehoiakim, son of Josiah; reigned eleven years (609–598).
3. Jehoiachin, son of Jehoiakim; reigned three months (598).
4. Zedekiah, Josiah's brother; reigned eleven years (598–587).

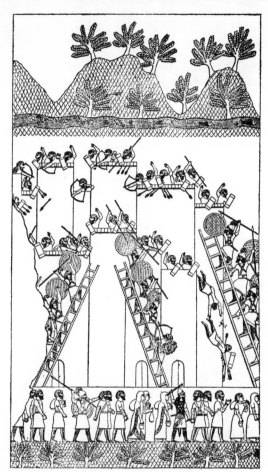

Central section: attack on a stronghold.
Bottom section: convoy of prisoners.

God, the pagans have invaded your heritage [Jerusalem],
they have descrated your holy Temple
they have reduced Jerusalem to a pile of ruins,
they have left the corpses of your servants
to the birds of the air for food,
and the flesh of your devout to the beasts of the earth. . . .

May the groans of the captive reach you;
by your mighty arm rescue those doomed to die!

(Ps. 178)

143

distance to the south. As a result he retained control of Judah which thus became Egypt's vassal.

The elders of Jerusalem had placed on the throne Jehoahaz, Josiah's eldest son. Neco, who did not trust this prince, summarily deposed him and deported him to Egypt. Jehoahaz reigned scarcely three months (609).

On Neco's orders Jehoahaz was replaced by his brother Jehoiakim. At the beginning of his reign the new sovereign seemed to have decided to be an obedient vassal; with great regularity he paid the enormous tribute exacted by Egypt.

Between 609 and 606 Nebupolassar and his son Nebuchadnezzar were busy fighting in Armenia. Directly they had concluded their business with the northern rebels they came down towards the Euphrates. In passing they halted at Haran where, as was related above, the last enclave of Assyrian resistance, which had escaped from Nineveh, was entrenched. The matter was soon settled. The huge Assyrian power, which for several centuries had held sway over the east, thus disappeared unobtrusively from the military history of western Asia.

Nebuchadnezzar, the hereditary prince of Babylon, was in command of the Babylonian army. He was an outstanding tactician and inflicted a terrible defeat on the Egyptians, cutting them in pieces so that they were obliged to retreat in haste to the Delta (May–June, 605). The Babylonian forces pursued them at close quarters and would probably have finished them off altogether, but at this moment news came to Nebuchadnezzar of the death of his father in the palace at Babylon (15–16 August 605). Nebuchadnezzar had therefore to abandon the pursuit of his enemy to return as quick as he could to the capital of his empire.[26]

[26] Until quite recently, following the statements of ancient historians, it was thought that Nebuchadnezzar, on the heels of Neco, was nearing Pelusium 'the gateway to the Delta' when he received news of Nebupolassar's death. About

Nebuchadnezzar was in a hurry to return to Babylon to keep usurpers off the throne. He had only to put in an appearance to receive the crown.

Thus, Judah, formerly the vassal of Egypt for a few years under Neco, became in 605 the vassal of the Babylonian empire. It was at this point that things began seriously to go wrong.

Jehoiakim, the vassal of Nebuchadnezzar, king of Babylon (606–603)

This new Babylonian empire lasted for a relatively short time, only eighty years in round figures (616–539). The forty-two years of Nebuchadnezzar's reign (604–562) occupied well over half of this period. He was a military genius who distinguished himself by extraordinary exploits throughout the Middle East, but he was also an excellent administrator and a tireless builder: he was able, in fact, to transform his capital city of Babylon into one of the finest cities of the ancient world. In addition, his haughty authoritarianism did not allow his satellite states to take the slightest liberty. In view of the rather turbulent character of the sovereigns of Judah conflicts semed inevitable in the near future. The tragedy was, in the circumstances, that the military party in Jerusalem did not realize that a declaration of war on this huge empire was nothing less than absolute suicide.

It might have been hoped that Judah would be integrated into the new political organization without too

ten years ago the deciphering of certain Babylonian chronicles preserved at the British Museum have resulted in a correction of this statement. According to these chronicles, which are written on bricks, Nebuchadnezzar was not on the frontiers of Egypt when he decided to return to Babylon. In reality he was camping near Homs in Syria about 500 miles from his capital to which he returned by traversing the Arabian wilderness, without baggage and with a very small escort mounted on two camels. He took the caravan route leading to Babylon by way of Palmyra and Hit. (*Nova Chronica babylonica* – Tabula British Museum 21946 – Chronica Wiseman: 605–595a. C – Pugna apud Karkemis et expugnation Syriae mart. – Aug. 605. In *Biblica* 1956, vol. 37, fasc. 3, pp. 388–9.)

much difficulty. Jehoiakim seemed disposed to accept the new state of affairs, and as a matter of fact there was a brief period of peace in Judah.

The future of Yahwism, nonetheless, gave cause for disquiet. Jehoiakim *did what is displeasing to Yahweh, just as his ancestors had done* (2 Kings 23:37), notes the biblical writer. The prophet Jeremiah informs us more explicitly about the serious dangers threatening the national religion in the near future. They can be classified under three principal categories — syncretism, formalism, fetishism.

Syncretism: the Judaeans did not reject the worship of Yahweh, but they combined with it the worship given to other gods, to the Baals, Ashtoreth, the idols with human or animal faces.

Formalism: scarcely anyone at the time of Jehoiakim thought of basing their conduct on the 'Second Law' revealed to his people by Josiah hardly twenty years previously. Religion of the heart, the conversation of the Lord's faithful follower with him, intimate, personal prayer, save for a few exceptions, were hardly thought of. It was very simple and far more practical to confine religion to the ancient sacrificial rite; the individual placed on the altar the usual offering (an animal or a symbolic part of the harvest) and he then thought that God was strictly obliged to grant what he asked. It was the still living memory of a magic rite which originated at a remote period. What was important in the circumstances was the kind of animal offered, its age and physical condition and, of course, the exact performance of the complicated rites. It seemed as if the people were still in the centuries of the times before Abraham when the shepherds of the plains offered their sacrifices before their primitive idols.

Fetishism: regarding his personal future and that of

his nation the Judaean was quite without misgivings. In the capital city of Jerusalem stood the Temple where Yahweh dwelt. It was a shrine regarded as inviolable. It was unthinkable that an enemy of the Chosen People should capture the City of David and penetrate into Yahweh's sanctuary.

That was the position: false views and very dangerous ones, combined with a childish theology. Jeremiah opposed these errors with all his strength, denouncing them with great vehemence.

Jeremiah had stood out as the enthusiastic collaborator of Josiah in his great religious reform; he now showed himself the declared opponent of the successors of this same Josiah. He spoke against all these sovereigns who were leading the country to disaster, attacking their baleful policies. Jeremiah was a man of affectionate nature who would have liked a calm and untroubled life, and yet the whole time he was sent by Yahweh to fight against kings, priests and the people. And so his meditations from time to time are punctuated with despair:

'A curse on the day when I was born'
(Jer. 20:14).

In the fourth year of Jehoiakim's reign (that is, in 605) the struggle between the young king and the prophet began. Jeremiah had decided to take a scroll and write on it all the prophecies that he had so far pronounced against Jerusalem. Then he ordered his secretary, Baruch, to go and read this scroll, probably not very pleasant hearing for the inhabitants of Jerusalem, before the people assembled in the Temple for a festival. The effect was overwhelming; all present were filled with terror. The officials present thought that the scroll should be taken to the king and he ordered that it should be read to him. It was wintertime – the month of *Chislev,* which corresponds to December – and the king was sitting by

Baruch son of Neriah duly carried out the order that the prophet Jeremiah had given him, to read all the words of Yahweh from the book in his Temple. He read the words of Jeremiah from the book . . . where all the people could hear.

Jeremiah 36:8–10

a brazier. When he had heard three or four columns of these prophecies, Jehoiakim, filled with rage, began to cut the scroll in pieces with a knife and then throw the pieces angrily into the fire.

At the end the whole of the manuscript was burned. Beside himself, Jehoiakim ordered the arrest of Jeremiah and Baruch, but they had prudently taken flight.

It was a bad beginning to the relationship between the king and the prophet.

For three years (605–602) Jehoiakim gave every appearance of being Nebuchadnezzar's eager and respectful vassal. In reality he was secretly plotting with Egypt which, as usual, was continually urging Judah to throw off the Babylonian yoke. Jeremiah was well aware of these secret manoeuvres and thought them extremely dangerous.

Thus two parties were in confrontation in Jerusalem. There were the warmongers, led by the king himself, who impatiently awaited the favourable moment for open rebellion against Nebuchadnezzar; there were those who were for peace, for whom Jeremiah was the untiring and vehement spokesman.

The prophet was sure that he would never convince the king. Moreover the die was cast. Yahweh had decided to mete out exemplary punishment on the king who had refused to heed the religious warnings of Yahweh's envoy and was determined to *follow other gods*. As a result of this, Jeremiah openly declared, Nebuchadnezzar, king of Babylon, would be sent by Yahweh to Jerusalem: *'The whole land of Judah shall be devastated and reduced to a desert, while they will stay in slavery among the nations for seventy years* (Jer. 25:11). *Only when the seventy years granted to Babylon are over, will I visit you.* (Jer. 29:10). The prophecy was indeed a terrible one.

The word that was addressed to Jeremiah by Yahweh, 'Get up and make your way down to the potter's house . . .' And whenever the vessel he was making came out wrong . . . he would start afresh and work it into another vessel . . . 'House of Israel, can not I do to you what this potter does? – it is Yahweh who speaks. Yes, as clay is in the potter's hand, so you are in mine, House of Israel.'

Jeremiah 18 : 1–6

These are the words of the book written in Babylon by Baruch son of Neraiah, son of Mahseiah, son of Zedekiah, son of Hasadiah, son of Hilkiah, in the fifth year, on the seventh day of the month, at the time when the Chaldaeans captured Jerusalem and burned it down.

Baruch 1 : 1–2

Jeremiah's campaign against any warlike action was illustrated by picturesque examples and symbolic actions intended to strike the imagination of his hearers. One day, probably in about 605, we find him going down to a potter's house while the latter was working at the wheel. The prophet then told his hearer this fable: when the vessel came out wrong from the hands of the potter he broke and threw it away for scrap. Then he begins another. This is how Yahweh will act if the Chosen People, the work of God, do not mend its ways (Jer. 18).

On another occasion, also about 605, he gathered together a small group in which were some of the priests of the Temple; the party went down towards one of the gates of the city called the Potherd's gate. There, in the name of the God of Israel, Jeremiah reminded them of the iniquities committed by Judah; incense offered to foreign gods, the abandonment of the worship of Yahweh, the sacrifice of innocent children in the flames. He then foretold the punishment to come: *'I* [Yahweh speaking through the mouth of his prophet] *will make this city a desolation, a derision; . . . I will make them eat the flesh of their own sons and daughters: they shall eat each other during the siege, in the shortage to which their enemies in their determination to kill them will reduce them.'* In conclusion the prophet took an earthenware jug which he had brought with him and broke it: it was thus that Jerusalem would be destroyed.

Jeremiah went at once to the court of the Temple where he spoke sharply to the people: *'Yahweh Sabaoth, the God of Israel, says this, "Yes, I am going to bring down every disaster I have threatened on this city"'* (Jer. 19).

Jeremiah had gone too far. The priest Pashhur, who was in charge of the police of the Temple, ordered the arrest of the prophet; then he had him beaten and put in stocks at the Gate of Benjamin, in which ignominious position he remained until next day. But directly he was set free Jeremiah continued his frightening predictions: the City of David and all Judah would fall into the hands of the king of Babylon; Pashhur and his minions would be deported to the banks of the Euphrates and they would never return from this far-off country (Jer. 20).

Jehoiakim's rebellion against Nebuchadnezzar (602–598)

In 602 Jehoiakim came out into the open; he refused to pay the tribute that he was obliged to send annually to Babylon. To bring the rebel to heel Nebuchadnezzar did no more than send a small contingent of regular troops together with armed bands of Chaldaeans, Arameans, Moabites and Ammonites to lay waste the country (2 Kings 24:2).

A little later the king of Babylon decided to go in person to make the petty king see reason; he marched on Jerusalem.

There was feverish activity in the city. On the one hand there was the military party who despite successive dissappointments still counted on an Egyptian alliance and made ready to break with Babylon. On the other side was a party for peace, under Jeremiah, and probably supported by other prophets. The prophet Habakkuk may have been one of them. In the streets of Jerusalem and at the gates of the city Jeremiah strenuously preached non-resistance, submission to Babylon and strict neutrality. Judah must accept the overlordship of Babylon as the lesser evil. Jerusalem must be beware of the Egyptian promises. A declaration of war against Babylon was absolute madness, Jeremiah explained to his audience; so rash a policy could have no other result than the impending and complete destruction of Jerusalem.

Jehoiakim reacted vigorously. He had to rid himself

of the opposition party and strong measures were needed. The king flooded Jerusalem *with innocent blood* (2 Kings 24:4). In other words a period of persecution of the prophets began.

To escape this organized repression Jeremiah must have had powerful protectors at the palace, and indeed less and less did he scruple to propagate his views with vehemence:

> *'I will reduce you* (Jerusalem) . . .
> *to an uninhabited town.'*   (Jer. 22:6)

Even the king was reviled: Jeremiah foretold a dreadful death for him and a mockery of a funeral:

> *'Doom for that man!*
> *He will receive the funeral honours of a donkey,* [27]
> *– dragged away and thrown*
> *out of the gates of Jerusalem.'*   (Jer. 22:18–19)

In December 598, Jehoiakim died at the eary age of thirty-six (2 Kings 24:6).

Jehoiakim's son was hurriedly placed on the throne with the name of Jehoiachin.

Shortly afterwards (January 597) Nebuchadnezzar arrived outside the walls of Jerusalem and began the siege.

Jerusalem and its three months of siege

Jehoiachin, the new king, was eighteen (2 Kings 24:8). [28] He was without experience of government and was surrounded by bad advisors who made him follow his father's policy. *He did what is displeasing to Yahweh, just as his father had done.* He was another protector of the Baals and the idols.

---

[27] That is, his corpse would be left out in the open air in a field outside the city, as was done with the decaying carcass of a domestic animal.

[28] And not eight as given in 2 Chron, 36:9, probably owing to a scribe's error.

The siege lasted for three months. Supporters of the war expected the Egyptians to appear on the scene from one moment to the next, and to see the Babylonian army and Nebuchadnezzar thrown back ignominiously to the Euphrates. Their hope was vain. As usual, Egypt always ready to urge Judah to rebellion, did not move.

Jerusalem could not hold out for long. The second day of the month of *Adar* (15–16 March 597) Jehoiachin determined to surrender to his powerful enemy. Probably the young king in his naïveté imagined that his prompt submission would earn him fairly easy peace terms. But Nebuchadnezzar decided to make an example of him.

The first[29] deporation of Judaeans to Babylon (597)
Nebuchadnezzar therefore refused to leave Jehoiachin on the throne as his vassal. He was to be deported to Babylon. The Old Testament and the cuneiform Chronicle supplement each other on this subject. In the convoy which set off to Babylon were the king, his harem, his mother, and his domestic and military establishment. There were about 10,000 deported (2 Kings 24:14), in the following categories: 7,000 men able to bear arms, 1,222 *blacksmiths and metalworkers*.[30] The rest were made up of 'nobles and notables'. In the country districts *only the poorest people were left behind*. In Jerusalem, also, a certain number of important persons continued to reside there, among others Jeremiah.

And so Jehoiachin was deported in chains with his

[29] There were three successive deportations to Babylon. They are dealt with here as they occur chronologically. The following is a summary list of them:
1. In 597, in the reign of Jehoiachin.
2. In 587, at the end of the reign of Zedekiah.
3. In 582, after the murder of Gedaliah.

[30] These metalworkers were rather scarce in the ancient east; in this instance they were taken to Babylon either to paralyse the arsenals of Jerusalem or to strengthen the teams of metalworkers for whom the Babylonians had a pressing need for their armament. The two hypotheses are not contradictory.

family to Babylon. He remained there thirty-seven years until his death — as Jeremiah had foretold, when, in the name of Yahweh, he spoke as follows: *'I will deliver you into the hands of . . . Nebuchadnezzar king of Babylon, the hands of the Chaldaeans. You and the mother who bore you, I will thrust you both out into another country; you were not born there but you will die there'* (Jer. 22:25–26).

In the next chapter we shall again encounter this pitiable caravan on its way to Babylon and witness the establishment of the prisoners in the region assigned to them. For the moment we must follow the course of events in Canaan.

In Jerusalem Nebuchadnezzar seized all the treasure of the royal palace and the Temple. He broke up all the gold furnishings which Solomon had collected in the House of Yahweh. Thus was fulfilled the extraordinary prophecy made by Isaiah to Hezekiah: *'The days are coming when everything in your palace, everything that your ancestors have amassed until now, will be carried off to Babylon'* (2 Kings 2:14).[31]

During this same campaign in Canaan, Nebuchadnezzar seized Lachish, an important stronghold which afforded protection on the side of the Egyptian frontier

V. Reign of Zedekiah, last king of the line of David (597–587)

Before returning to Babylon Nebuchadnezzar replaced the unhappy Jehoiachin by Zedekiah, the brother of Josiah. He was twenty-one, of less than second-rate mind, with no ideas of his own and lacking any intellectual power at all. He allowed himself to be influenced by the pro-Egyptian and anti-Babylonian party. Like

---

[31] In this case there can be no question of a *prophetia post eventum;* Isaiah's inimitable style dates the passage with certainty.

his predecessors he continued to hope foolishly that he would succeed in regaining the freedom of Judah. In the last resort it was Jerusalem which was to be broken, finally, like the earthenware vessel which Jeremiah shattered at the gate of the Potsherd.

In Jerusalem: the war party and the peace party with the king between them

Deportation of the unfortunate Jehoiachin did nothing to calm political passions in Jerusalem. With increased violence the war party confronted the partisans of peace. Between the two, undecided and timid, was the new king of Judah, Zedekiah (597–587)

The military party eagerly resumed more or less secret conversations with the other vassal nations of Babylon (Edom, Ammon, Moab, Tyre, Sidon) which were impatient to shake off the Babylonian yoke. They plotted together almost openly and endeavoured to bring Egypt into their plans; but ever since the severe lesson he had been taught at Carchemish, Neco II (609–593) while insidiously urging the discontented countries to rebel, took good care not to commit himself to a real offensive alliance. After him, Psammetichus II (593–588) pursued the same shrewd policy. Despite this, in Jerusalem the war party felt sure that when the moment came Egypt would fight, and they looked forward calmly and confidently to a renewal of hostilities.

The prophets, under the untiring leadership of Jeremiah, continued to preach submission to Nebuchadnezzar. They did so in the formal interests of the nation. It was, of course, true that the annual tribute to be paid to Babylon was very heavy, but in this way Judah was to all intents and purposes free, in practice, if not in theory. Another uprising against Babylon could obviously have no other consequence than the destruction of Jerusalem and its population.

Then, too, the mission of the Chosen People did not consist in dissipating its energies in useless political and military contests; the lofty role reserved to it was the thorough study, meditation and practice of the Law.

To endeavour to convince his fellow-citizens Jeremiah continually went through the streets explaining the situation and showing the people and their leaders where their responsibilities lay. One day, to illustrate his remarks, he went round the principal streets of the city on hands and knees, a wooden yoke on his neck as a sign of the political yoke that the people of Jerusalem would have to bear if they clung obstinately to their insane plans.

The false prophet Hananaiah, who had previously foretold the return in two years' time of the first body of citizens to be deported, took Jeremiah's yoke and broke it in pieces. Shortly afterwards Jeremiah reappeared with an iron yoke and said: *'Yahweh Sabaoth, the God of Israel says this: "An iron yoke is what I now lay on the necks of all these nations to subject them to Nebuchadnezzar king of Babylon"'* (Jer. 28:14).

The wretched Zedekiah was torn between these two irreconcilable parties, but he felt attracted more strongly by the movement favouring rebellion which asserted that it could obtain the liberation of the country. On the other hand, he felt great reverence for the prophet, who nonetheless in his public speeches did not spare the king and continually and vehemently inveighed against him.

The beginning of the revolt of Jerusalem against Nebuchadnezzar (589)

It was Egypt which tipped the balance.

With Neco and Psammetichus the Egyptian empire pursued a policy of non-intervention in Asia. But directly after the death of Psammetichus, Hophra, brother of the dead king (*Apries* of the Greek historians), announced that he was ready to join the coalition of the vassal nations; he formally undertook to give full military support to the expedition intended to destroy Babylon.

Hostilities opened in the very year of Hophra's accession. Using the island of Tyre, his new ally, as a naval base, he sent a contingent to Phoenicia by sea to occupy the rear and thus block the route to be taken by Nebuchadnezzar when he made for Jerusalem. Thus his advance would be considerably delayed (or so his opponents hoped) and Hophra in this way would gain time to mobilize the main body of his troops in Egypt.

Nebuchadnezzar's lightning counterstroke (588)

Without losing a moment Nebuchadnezzar, at the head of a large army, took the field. He began by establishing his headquarters at Riblah on the Orontes.

He had decided on his plan of campaign: first he would swoop down on Jerusalem and besiege it. Dividing his army he would send a part into Phoenicia which wold be promptly brought to see reason; he would continue the siege of Jerusalem and when he had captured the city would attack Egypt and annex it.

That was the plan of this amazing tactician and, except for the part of it concerning Egypt, it was all realized.

The siege of Jerusalem (January 588–June-July 587)

It lasted eighteen months.

The inhabitants of Jerusalem thought that their citadel was practically impregnable. Its position on a steep rock with an almost sheer drop on three sides, has already been described. Down the centuries the kings of

Judah carried out many improvements to the defences; by Zedekiah's time Jerusalem bristled with ramparts. All the defenders had to do was to hold out until the arrival of Hophra's Egyptian troops who would soon put Nebuchadnezzar to flight.

The latter had made an entrenchment all round the city to prevent it receiving supplies from outside.

To begin with, the morale of the population was excellent. But the Egyptian battalions, heralded so loudly, never arrived. Soon food began to be scarce because a certain number of country people had come to seek shelter behind the city's ramparts. At the end of a few months famine prevailed, and possibly the plague as well (Jer. 38:2). The situation was turning to tragedy.

The false prophets tried to uphold the people's courage by announcing daily the coming deliverance. But the reality gave the lie to these misleading promises.

Jeremiah, on the other hand, continued to thunder out his predictions of misfortune. He advised the king, officials, and private individuals to surrender as the only means of saving Jerusalem and its inhabitants. But the prophet's speeches were received with derision and sarcasm, and even threats. His anti-patriotic and, according to the ideas of the times, his anti-religious attitude soon made him suspect of treason; it began to be thought that this pessimistic speech-maker might be the leader of a band of traitors, in the pay of Nebuchadnezzar, entrusted with the task of undermining the moral resistance of the beleagured city.

And yet Jeremiah was the only one, or practically the only one, to have been right about the political situation. But his role became increasingly unbearable. By force of circumstances he soon came to be regarded as a dangerous spy whom it would be only prudent to get rid of as soon as possible.

Zedekiah visited the prophet secretly to ask his advice. The answer was unvarying: Jerusalem must open its gates to Nebuchadnezzar: *'If you go out and surrender to the officers of the king of Babylon your life will be safe and this city will not be burnt down. . . . But if you do not . . . this city will be handed over into the power of the king of the Chaldaeans who will burn it down; and you yourself will not escape their hands'* (Jer. 38:15–23). Royal protection, not worth a great deal after all, was powerless to save the prophet from all sorts of persecution which now befell him. He was interned in the Court of the Guard, then thrown into a well empty of water but half full of mud in which he would have ended his days had it not been for the help of the Ethiopian Ebed-melech, a eunuch of the royal palace.

Hope disappointed

For exactly a year, Nebuchadnezzar, having settled down before the fortifications of Jerusalem, patiently awaited his prey. Suddenly news came to the besieged, news that they scarcely dared hope for; Hophra had set out from Egypt with his army and even now was arriving to deliver the City of David. The joy of the inhabitants of Jerusalem may be imagined when they saw the Chaldaeans hurriedly raising the siege to march against the Egyptian troops; they waited eagerly for news of the Egyptian victory. They felt sure that Yahweh, in agreement with the powerful alien deities introduced into the Temple, would spare his people the shame of capitulation and the sacking of the capital. And they recalled Yahweh's amazing feat in the days of Hezekiah and Sennacherib, the miraculous deliverance of Jerusalem foretold by the prophet Isaiah (see page 105).

But the prophet Jeremiah appeared to have received a mission different from that of his predecessor. He proclaimed vehemently that the Chaldeans had raised the siege only for the time being; the battle that they would fight with the Egyptians would end with the total defeat of the latter and very soon Nebuchadnezzar and his troops would be seen returning in triumph more threatening than ever; the siege would be continued and would end in the fall of Jerusalem (Jer. 37:7–10).

And this was the course taken by events. Hophra's army, cut in pieces, was obliged to return to its Egyptian bases in disorder. Nebuchadnezzar did not pursue it further. His primary concern was to finish his business with the insufferable Judaean capital and strike it from the map.

The elders and military leaders began to see that Jeremiah was right. Nonetheless he was thrown into prison in an underground cell where he spent several weeks.

The siege went on. In the capital conditions began to grow really very bad indeed. There were epidemics and famine (Lam. 1:20). Men came to envy the fate of those who fell in the skirmishes. Even the wealthy, living skeletons, dropped down dead in the streets. Mothers killed their children, cooked and ate them (Lam. 2:20; 4:10).

The end of Jerusalem: ninth day of the fourth month (June–July 587)

With their efficient engines of war the Chaldaeans succeeded in opening a breach in the ramparts. The Chaldaean troops burst into the city (Jer. 39:2; 52:5–7; 2 Kings 25:2–4). The king of Babylon's officers, Nergal-sharezer, prince of Sin-magin, and the high official Nebushazban established their quarters at the Middle Gate.

Under cover of darkness, Zedekiah and a small group of warriors attempted flight. They hoped to be able to

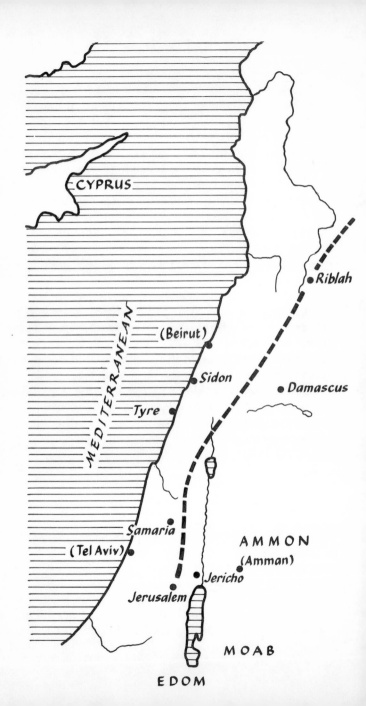

get to Egypt or Ammon by skirting the Dead Sea. They left the city by way of the king's garden to the south of the ramparts; but a Chaldaean patrol was on their heels and came up with them very quickly on the way to Jericho. Zedekiah was captured.

He was taken at once to Riblah, Nebuchadnezzar's headquarters, on whose orders Zedekiah's sons were put to death in their father's presence. This was the last thing seen by the unfortunate king, for directly after this his eyes were put out. He was then sent to Babylon in chains.

Jerusalem was given over to the soldiers; they searched and plundered the houses, they killed the old, the adult men and the youths; they raped the women (Lam. 5:11).

A month after the sacking of Jerusalem, Nebuzaradan, commander of the royal guard, received orders to carry out a final act of vengeance for the Judaean rebellion. Seventy men of importance – priests and notables – were taken to Riblah where they were put to death. In addition, in the Temple Court great numbers of executions were carried out. The Temple itself was savagely desecrated. A band of Babylonians was ordered to seize the golden, silver and bronze vessels used for worship. Jeremiah

---

FALL OF JERUSALEM (587 B.C.)
END OF THE KINGDOM OF JUDAH

In the fourth year of his reign Zedekiah, king of Jerusalem, allowed himself to be dragged into a plot by Edom, Moab, Ammon, Tyre and Sidon against Nebuchadnezzar, king of Babylon (604–562). Jeremiah opposed the signature of this pact which, he foretold, would cause great misfortunes. The Babylonian armies came to besiege the City of David. Nebuchadnezzar raised the siege temporarily to go out against the Egyptian army which had come to the help of the beleagured city. Cut in pieces, the Egyptians were obliged to return to the Delta. When the food in the capital was exhausted Zedekiah attempted to leave the city in secret together with a group of his soldiers. He was caught near Jericho and taken prisoner. He was put in chains and taken to Riblah. There his sons were put to death in his presence; his eyes were put out and he was then taken to Babylon. Jerusalem fell into the power of Nebuchadnezzar.

gives a long list of them: ash containers, scoops, knives, the sprinkling bowls, the incense boats . . . the large vessels like the Sea of Bronze, the bronze pillars of Jachin and Boaz. These were all broken up and the pieces carefully packed and sent off to Babylon. After these depradations the Temple and the royal palace were burned to the ground. The same was done for the finest of the private houses. The ramparts were also torn down, stone by stone. Only the houses in the poorer districts still stood. For thirty days the Babylonians burned what they could not carry off with them to the banks of the Euphrates.

Thus were fulfilled the prophecies of Jeremiah who in Yahweh's name had declared:

> *'I will make Jerusalem*
> *a heap of stones,*
> *a haunt of jackals,*
> *. . . A desert*
> *with none to live there.*   (Jer. 10:10)

> *Mount Zion is desolate;*
> *jackals roam to and fro on it.'*
>
> (Lam. 5:18)

Second deportation (587)

The first deportation to Babylon, ordered by Nebuchadnezzar in 597 in the time of Jehoiachin had taken 10,000 men from Jerusalem.

The second deportation, with which we are now concerned, numbered according to Jeremiah (and this is the only figure given in the Bible) 832 persons from Jerusalem. Biblical scholars regard this number as rather too small to be taken seriously.

Nebuchadnezzar allowed Jeremiah, whom the conquerors had freed from prison, to choose his own place of residence; he was free, if he liked, to follow the exiles into Babylon or he could stay in Jerusalem. In reply he said that he would stay in Judah. He had in fact determined to work for the material and especially the spiritual restoration of the country.

It should not be thought that the whole country had been entirely laid waste. Here and there some rural centres remained and a few farms which slowly returned to life. And although in Jerusalem the wealthy parts of the city had been burned down, the poor quarters which held no interest for the soldiers in their desire for plunder emerged almost unscathed from the trial. Thus amid all the ruin there was a nucleus of a city which began to take shape once more.

There can be little doubt about the moral condition of this small human group, bewildered, disconcerted and leaderless; they were ripe, it is obvious, to seek the consolations of the most primitive religion. It appears that even the memory of Yahweh would shortly disappear from what had been called the 'Promised Land'.

Jeremiah, now an old man, took his place beside Gedaliah, a faithful Yahwist whom Nebuchadnezzar had appointed governor of what remained of the kingdom of Judah. With his habitual fervour he desired to devote himself enthusiastically to the pacification and spiritual restoration of the country. The new administrative centre had been established not in Jerusalem but at Mizpah, a short distance from the city. And there we find Jeremiah working hard, devoting himself body and soul to the material and moral restoration of his unfortunate co-religionists.

There were still some centres of resistance. Ammon and Moab did their best to stir up the political passions of those Judaeans thirsting for revenge. In great secrecy an assassination was plotted. Gedaliah, after scarcely two months in power, was murdered by these fanatics.

The whole country was at once seized with panic. The consequences of this crime could easily be foreseen, for Nebuchadnezzer would certainly repress without mercy this attempt against his sovereign rights; once more terrible punishments could be expected. As a last resort, it might be better, the people were beginning to think, to flee from the anger of Nebuchadnezzer and seek refuge in Egypt, in a quieter region where a new life could be started. Jeremiah, consulted on the matter, was against leaving the country. Yahweh, he said, required the Judaeans to remain in the land of their fathers; very soon, he explained, the Chosen People would again take root in this land which had been solemnly given to Abraham; after so many misfortunes Israel would experience, in Judah, times of unequalled prosperity and Yahweh would heap blessings on the sons of Jacob. But the headstrong people would not believe the prophet's revelations; Jeremiah was accused of falsifying Yahweh's messages. They were determined to leave the country. A sizable body of Judaeans hurriedly set out for Egypt. One of the groups took the prophet Jeremiah with them by force. In the circumstances his vociferous protests can be imagined.

A party of these voluntary exiles settled at Tahpanhes in the Nile Delta near Pelusium. Shortly afterwards another was established at Migdol, a little to the east. Others pushed on to Memphis (which the Bible calls Noph) in lower Egypt. A fourth contingent went as far as the land of Pathros in Upper Egypt (Jer. 44:1).

In his new residence at Tahpanhes Jeremiah experienced great grief in seeing his fellow-countrymen worship various idols, particularly the Queen of Heaven, a goddess whom the Judaeans regarded as the female equivalent of Yahweh. They had gone too far. The unhappy prophet foretold the imminent punishment of the idolaters. In this very place, one day Nebuchadnezzar would appear and punish the apostates severely (the prediction referred to the lightning-like campaign of 568–567 in the time of Pharaoh Amasis).

There is a tradition, which seems by no means unlikely, and is mentioned by Tertullian and St Jerome that, infuriated by Jeremiah's threats and reproaches, the Judaeans stoned him to death.

Thus disappeared this attractive personality who since Josiah's time had always been a prominent figure. At first sight it might be thought that Jeremiah had been defeated in the immense effort that he made to save Jerusalem from destruction. He had denounced all the internal and external dangers threatening Judah; he had warned his fellow-countrymen in clear terms, against their religious errors and political mistakes which, since Josiah's death had been very numerous. Faced with their continued obstinacy he had foretold the unprecedented punishment which would fall upon the kingdom.

His failure was only apparent. It is true that he had been unable to bring Israel back to the pure worship of Yahweh; he had not succeeded in persuading the rulers to adopt the strict policy of neutrality that was then necessary. It remains true, nonetheless, that the spiritual influence of his preaching on centuries to come was of the first importance. This prophet who seems so hard, so vehement, was, as we know from what he tells us, a timid and affectionate person. Throughout his life, on Yahweh's orders, Jeremiah never married; and so he had no child to comfort him in his old age. Yahweh had forbidden him to take part in public rejoicing and he suffered very much at being accused of loving neither his native land nor his religion; he cried out his discouragement to the Lord and felt at every moment that he must give up his mission, but in the end he obeyed the commanding voice which brought him back to his duty, to the thick of the fight.

And then, when all seemed lost, he foretold the wonderful future awaiting Israel. From an earthly point of view all had collapsed. But the prophet had understood that the kingdom of God is not realized here below by territorial conquests. All empires fall to pieces, one after the other, in the clash of arms. But the aim of the faithful Yahwist is not the pursuit of the wealth of this world but the attempt to live in close fellowship with God.

That is the enduring spiritual message of the great prophet. And we shall find it taken to heart more thoroughly still by the Babylonian Exiles.

The third and last deportation to Babylon (582)

After the murder of Gedaliah, and while Jeremiah was spending the last of his days so unhappily in Egypt, the dreaded reaction came quickly enough. The unfortunate Judaeans who had remained in the land of their fathers were to pay once again, and severely, for the criminal blunders of their politicians. On this occasion the repression was undertaken by Nebuzaradan, the Chaldaean commander whom we have already encountered. According to a short note of Jeremiah's, 745 people were deported to Babylon this time.

Judah had been bled white. All its people, willingly or unwillingly, but most under threat of violence, had left the Promised Land. Jerusalem was no more than a semi-wilderness, occupied by a few hovels on a corner of the rock. What had become of the times of David the glorious or Solomon the magnificent? In the desolate country-side there were still a few hamlets, decimated by the passing of armies and the merciless commandeering of manpower, which eked out a precarious existence. Logically, the early and complete disappearance of this remnant of Judah could be predicted. In addition, the immediate neighbours, the Edomites and Ammonites, invaded these almost uninhabited territories.

But the course of the history of the People of God is entirely unlike that of other civilizations. When it had reached the very depths, the 'remnant of Israel' was able at last to see clearly within itself. From this Babylonian Exile which in all logic should have been its downfall, its complete destruction, it was to emerge regenerated, — stronger, more living, more luminous than ever.

6

THE EXILE IN BABYLON (597–536)

After the death of Solomon there followed three and a half centuries (931–597) of continual tragedy, the price paid for a senseless domestic and foreign policy. The punishment was severe: in 721 came the fall of Samaria, the capital of the northern kingdom (see Map, page 66) and the complete disapearance of the Ten Tribes of Israel; in 587, there was the fall of Jerusalem, the capital of the southern kingdom, the massacre of a great part of Judah and, finally, the deportation of the pick of the people to Babylon.

It certainly looked as if, historically, the Chosen People were doomed to complete destruction in a very short time. For Mesopotamia is a crucible in which were mingled and amalgamated populations of very diverse origins, working on the banks of the Two Rivers as prisoners of war under the orders of their conquerors. The Judaeans, it might have been thought, would shortly come under the influence of the common law and sooner or later be absorbed into this cosmopolitan milieu.

But it never happened. This group from Jerusalem set up a solid moral barrier against the foreign influences which threatened their traditions and religion. And so we see the formation of a kernel of implacable resistance to any form of assimilation. Through the terrible trials which the survivors of the siege of Jerusalem went through these unfortunate people were led to meditate in their hearts on the lessons of the past. As a result there came that great spiritual progress which found expression in an ardent study of the Law, a deepening of their understanding of the revelations of the prophets, the scrupulous observance of the commandments and the quest of and interior religion which would place its faithful followers in fervent contact with Yahweh. The Temple, of course, was no more; but to compensate in some sort for the disappearance of ritual sacrifice (which could only take place in the court of the sanctuary at Jerusalem) the Scriptures were searched with new fervour.

It was a real regeneration of Yahwism and the beginning of an unprecedented period of spiritual progress. It was the origin of a new era which the historians term Judaism; it was, in actual fact, a defensive institutional organization of monotheism against the dangers, attacks and inroads of paganism.

The number of Judaeans deported to Babylonia

On this point the Bible provides very imprecise, incomplete and sometimes contradictory information. And the cuneiform texts do not mention it.

The following are the figures taken from relevant chapters of the Bible:

First deportation under Jehoiachin. In 2 Kings 24:12 we are told that the first body of prisoners amounted to 10,000 sent into exile. A few lines further down (verse 16) there is a different figure, 8,000. Jeremiah (52:29) gives 3,023.

The second deportation after the fall of Jerusalem (587). Jeremiah here speaks of 832 exiles; this seems a very small number if, as seems to have been the case, Nebuchadnezzar determined to inflict an exemplary punishment on the ever rebellious Judaean capital.

The third and last deportation, in 582. Here again, according to Jeremiah, our only source of information, Nebuzaradan, Nebuchadnezzar's commander of the guard, deported 745 Judaeans to Babylon.

According to these figures and taking the highest for the first deportation, a total of 11,577 (10,000 + 832 + 745) were sent into exile.

Scholars who have specialized in the study of this period, referring to large-scale operations of the same kind as performed firstly by the Assyrians and, later, by the Chaldaeans, emphasize that enumerations of this kind do not include either women or children, or even servants. To obtain an idea of the size of a group of prisoners the total given above should be multiplied by a coefficient of four or five. This gives a grand total of between 50,000 and 60,000 exiles.

But some authors take as the basis of their calculations the smallest numbers given in the biblical text, namely, 3,023 .. 832 .. 745, that is in all 4,600 men. Multiplying by four we obtain the approximate figure of 20,000 prisoners for the three deportations.

According to the same authorities, before the deportation Judah contained a little over 100,000 inhabitants (something like 80 inhabitants to the square mile; total area of the territory about 1200 square miles). It is thus estimated that about threequarters of the Judaeans remained in their home country.

We need not dwell at length on this difficult and important question. Careful reading of the relevant biblical texts would seem to show that Judah was terribly impoverished both by war and deportations and it seems that the larger part of the manpower of the nation, both

in quantity and quality, took the road to exile on Nebuchadnezzar's orders.

The journey into exile

The Chaldaean bas-reliefs inform us clearly enough about
the terrible conditions of the prisoners' journey. More-
over, before the Babylonians, the Assyrians depicted
the prisoners on their way in the same manner.

The men had their arms tied so that their elbows were
touching behind their backs. Sometimes the prisoners
were chained two together, the left wrist of one attached
to his travelling companion's right wrist. Once they were
far enough away from their country of origin their chains
were removed. The women were not bound at all and
they are usually depicted sitting beside their young
children on two-wheeled carts; these vehicles, trans-
porting at the same time the clothes and the scanty
baggage, were of course drawn by the prisoners.

Journeys like this could last several months (Ezra 7:9).
Underfed, without the most elementary hygienic care,
and travelling most of the time under a blazing sun, the
prisoners sometimes fell exhausted on the plain. The
corpses of the unfortunate Judaeans lay along the tracks
leading to the banks of the Euphrates.

It is very probable that the columns of exiles took the
usual route through Aleppo; they then went down the
Euphrates as far as Babylon; a journey of about a thousand
miles of actual distance travelled.

Babylon, 'jewel and boast of the Babylonians' (Is. 13:19)

At last the wretched body of exiles was able to discern
shining white in the distance an enormous mass of
buildings dominated by a ziggurat (a staged tower)

about three hundred feet high. 'Bab-ilu', proudly announced the escorting soldiers. *Bab-ilu* meant 'the gate of God' — the god in question was Marduk, protector of the city.

It was totally unlike the Judaean cities huddled inside the ramparts with narrow twisted streets bordered with houses tightly packed together. Babylon was defended by a series of enclosures: enormous ramparts and impassable trenches. But the city itself, in the shape of an enormous trapezium crossed by the Euphrates, was laid out according to a plan that looks almost modern in inspiration and was huge and rectangular. The wide streets intersected at right angles; Babylon was an enormous checker board. The houses rose to three or four storeys, like those of Tyre.

Eight enormous gates gave access to the city. On arrival from the north, entrance was gained through the gate of Ishtar, magnificently adorned with thirteen superimposed layers of enamelled bricks in which blue was the predominant colour; archaeologists have counted 575 figures of bulls, dragons and fabulous animals. This gate was surmounted by a frieze which was also enamelled; the portico was crenellated.

From the Ishtar gate led the celebrated triumphal way (about half a mile long), paved with stone and bordered with royal palaces, defence works, temples, high walls adorned with glittering ceramics on which were represented enormous roaring lions. In one of the architectural features near the gate archaeologists believe that they have discovered the foundations of what were called the 'hanging gardens of Babylon' regarded by the ancients as one of the seven wonders of the world. Nebuchadnezzar had married a Persian princess and he had constructed a series of terraces in stages, supported on enormous arches, to remind her of the wooded, undulating countryside of her own land, on these terraces wonderful gardens had been made. Water for them was raised by mechanical means from the wells. Dominating the white mass of houses in the great city the green foliage of the palm trees proclaimed the glory of Nebuchadnezzar, builder and conqueror.

The triumphal way passed beside the enclosure wall of the temple of Marduk from which rose the ziggurat in its seven stages, known as the tower of Babel. Its square base had a side of nearly three hundred feet in length and the tower was over three hundred feet high.

About halfway along the triumphal way was an inter-section where it was joined by another avenue leading to the quays of the Euphrates and to the majestic bridge joining the two parts of the city. The pavement was formed of limestone slabs kept in place by pitch and on each slab at the edge of the road was carved the following inscription: 'It is I, Nebuchadnezzar, king of Babylon, son of Nebupolassar. I paved the street of Babylon with slabs of stone brought from the mountain for the pro-cession of the great god Marduk.'

On both banks of the river were wide quays for the unloading of merchandise arriving by river to *this land of merchants*, this *city of shopkeepers* (Ez. 17:4).

On all sides in the city there were temples (as many as fifty-three of them) of amazing size full of untold wealth. There were private houses with arrogant-looking facades. And in the outlying quarters, stood the workers' dwellings where the common people lived, the temple slaves, the prisoners of war, employed for building works, who laboured for this exacting oligarchy, the mistress of the Middle East.

So far, for reasons of clarity, the narrative has been confined to the events occurring in Jerusalem until the fall of the city to Nebuchadnezzar. Attention must now be turned to the lot of the exiles transported to Babylon in three successive deportations.

The lives of the Judaean exiles on the banks of the Euphrates can be divided into three periods.

At first, a period of thirty-five years (597–562), relatively arduous, and lasting from the first deportation (597) until the death of Nebuchadnezzar (562).

Then, from 562 until 549, some fiteen years during which Chaldaean supervision relaxed. The Judaeans lived in expectation of a liberator.

Lastly, from 548 until 538, ten years during which occurred the impatiently-awaited solution of their difficulty. 539: Fall of the Babylonian empire to the assaults of Cyrus, king of the Medes and Persians. 538: Edict of Cyrus authorizing the Judaean colony to return to its own country where the followers of Yahweh would be allowed to rebuild the Temple.

1. The life of the Judaean exiles in Babylon in the time of Nebuchadnezzar
(35 years: 597–562)

The Bible tells us very little about the living conditions of Jehoiachin, the fallen king, when in exile. Fortunately Chaldaean texts discovered at Babylon furnish us with information on this point. During the first quarter of the present century, an archaeological mission under the leadership of the eminent Assyriologist Robert Koldewey,[1] brought to light a considerable number of cuneiform inscriptions, especially in Nebuchadnezzar's summer

---

[1] The mission was under the auspices of the Deutsche Orient Gesellshaft, founded in Berlin in 1898. Excavations were begun in 1899 on the *tel* 'of Babil' (namely, the site of ancient Babylon). The work, which had gone on for eighteen years without interruption, had to be stopped in 1917 on account of the British advance on Mesopotamia. Koldewey is the greatest of the pioneers of Mesopotamian archaeology. There is a good summary of his work in Vol. I of *Archéologie mesopotamienne* by André Parrot.

palace. From this evidence E. F. Weidner[2] discovered that the name of Jehoiachin appeared in connection with various deliveries of foodstuffs, especially oil of sesame. The dethroned king is there termed 'king of Jadahu' (Judah). The decipherers noticed that the rations allotted to Jehoiachin were larger by far than those intended for his Judaean entourage, which was also lodged in the Chaldaean sovereign's palace.

Thus it appears that the prisoner was treated as a king by his captor.

Daily life of the Judaean prisoners

Very different, no doubt was the lot of prisoners of less exalted state.

Some of the Judaeans were employed perhaps in Babylon, but in any case quite close to the capital, where Nebuchadnezzar was undertaking important building operations. But the largest body of prisoners was settled near Nippur in the south of the country. From the prophet Ezekiel, who formed part of this contingent, we learn that the prisoners were *on the bank of the river Chebar*. Historians have identified this river with the Naru Kabaru of the cuneiform texts; it is one of the many irrigation canals taken from the Euphrates in this heavily cultivated region which was consecrated to Enlil, god of the earth. All this part of the country was criss-crossed with many canals for bringing water to the fields and horticultural establishments. The digging and maintenance of these little artificial rivers required numerous and properly qualified workers. Obviously the prisoners of war would have a place in this complex organization whose duty it was to open, shut and repair the sluices. It is in this sense

---

[2] 'Joakin, König von Juda, in babylonischen Kellsschriftentexten' in *Melanges syriens,* II, pp. 923–935. – See also, W. F. Albright, 'King Joiachin in Exile', in *The Biblical Archeologist,* 5, pp. 49–55.

that the well-known expression in Psalm 137 *(Super flumina Babylonis)* should be understood: *Beside the streams of Babylon*. We know the name of several of these villages in which the Judaeans were quartered: Tel-melah, Tel-harsha, Cherub, Addan, Immer (Ezr. 2:59), Casiphia (Ezr. 8:17) and Tel-Abib.[3] In these various places the exiles were not treated exactly as prisoners. But their movements were supervised, watched and controlled. Outside their work they enjoyed a certain freedom.

In the territory assigned to them the sons of Jacob lived in closed groups. They possessed their own organization and officials; their elders and elected notables could even pronounce sentence and see to the carrying out of their decrees.

By avoiding so far as possible all contact with the Chaldaeans and refusing to mix with the other exiles from different countries in Asia, they managed to preserve intact their national character. They were very probably grouped in clans, or at least, according to the different Palestinian villages from which they came, they lived as a family, and married within the Judaean group. In this wealthy country they led a far fuller life and one nothing like so hard as that which they had experienced in Canaan.

Without wishing in any way to minimize the moral and religious sufferings of the Exile, we are bound to admit that the material circumstances of the exiles, who were neither slaves nor serfs, must be regarded as very reasonable.

The spiritual state of the exiles

The religious position certainly appears to have been far less satisfactory.

[3] In Babylonian, *Tel-Abubi* (Tel of the flood). By alliteration the exiled called it: *Tel-Abib*, Tel of the ear of corn.

For ten years, from 597 to 587, that is, between the first and second deportation, the exiled Judaeans liked to believe that Yahweh would come providentially to their assistance before the final catastrophe; in their view the Temple of Jerusalem was the palladium of the City of David. Jeremiah felt obliged to write to them from Jerusalem to oppose this mistake, which was being preached throughout Babylon by false prophets who promised the exiles an early return to Jerusalem. Jeremiah warned what remained of the People of God against these illusions: the Exile, he told them, would last for a long time, for seventy years, to be precise. And he was lavish with his wise advice: *'Build houses, settle down; plant gardens and eat what they produce; take wives and have sons and daughters; choose wives for your sons, find husbands for your daughters so that these can bear sons and daughters in their turn; you must increase there and not decrease'* (Jer. 29:4–6).

So their trial was to continue; in fact it was only just at its beginning. Yahweh was making ready to send to his disobedient people the punishment that they deserved.

One day in 587 B.C. a survivor from Jerusalem arrived in Babylon to announce the capture of the city by Nebuchadnezzar's soldiers; the city had been pillaged and burned to the ground; the Temple was profaned and destroyed by fire. The City of David no longer existed.

For those weaker brethren who always hoped for a signal victory of the Egyptians over the Babylonian armies and dreamed of the glorious liberation of Jerusalem the blow was a terrible one; henceforward they had proof that Yahweh was not strong enough to protect his people; the Babylonian gods prevailed over the God of Abraham.

As a result, without completely giving up the worship of Yahweh, the Judaean exiles were increasingly inclined to invoke the gods of Mesopotamia. It was a further and very disquieting outbreak of syncretism.

But at this point help came from the prophet Ezekiel.

Ezekiel's message (duration of his ministry 593–570)

Ezekiel, who belonged to a priestly family, was among the first group of those deported. Three years after his arrival in the land of exile he saw a hand which was holding out a scroll to him; at the same time he heard a voice, telling him, *'son of man, eat this scroll, then go and speak to the House of Israel'* (Ezk. 3:1). This was a symbol of the divine message which he was to give to his co-religionists.

Ezekiel's message is one of great richness, but it is also very complex.

It seems that there were four messages.

Message regarding Israel's guilt: prediction of the punishments to be undergone by the People of God

Some of the Judaeans deported to Babylon seemed to think that they had been unjustly punished by God. Why did he treat his people so harshly when he ought, surely, to have dealt kindly with them? Ezekiel undertook to enlighten his proud and obstinate fellow-countrymen.

During the first six years of his ministry he tried to show his co-religionists how they were guilty in the sight of God. Repeating the fundamental teaching of Deuteronomy with some vehemence, the prophet blamed his companions for the acts of idolatry; he reminded them of the worship they had paid on the high places to the Asheras, the raised stones on which they had poured libations of wine or oil; he told them of Yahweh's anger for having burned their new-born children in criminal sacrifice; Israel, he proclaimed, was an unfaithful people; they would undergo a pnishment to match their sin. The kingdom of Judah would shortly experience the most terrible time of its whole history; Jerusalem would be destroyed; the Temple would be burned to the ground.

Hearing all these disasters predicted the exiles protested. Were the sons once more to pay for the sins of their fathers? Why should the exiles in Babylon suffer calamity because of the mistakes of their forbears? That was the cry of despair that went up from the exiles on the banks of the Euphrates.

On this point Ezekiel was able to comfort them a little. The old Israelite proverb

> *The fathers have eaten unripe grapes;*
> *and the children's teeth are set on edge,*

was obviously not applicable universally. The prophet preached the principle of personal responsibility, an idea which, after all, had never been entirely unknown in Israel. Nevertheless, in the circumstances it assumed the appearance of a solemn advance in the history of ideas and in the theological context.[4]

For this reason God would to some extent spare the innocent; they would be able to regroup and form the little 'remnant' so often mentioned by the prophets; and this 'remnant' would form the nucleus of the future Israel.

But for the time being, the exiles must get ready to suffer the most fearful trials.

---

[4] Note that the formulation of this principle does not put the theory of collective responsibility entirely out of court. Each individual is responsible for his own salvation while remaining, for his own part, responsible for the future salvation of his social group.

The proclamation of salvation

Time passed, Ezekiel's prophecies were fulfilled one by one, Jerusalem fell. Despair reigned among the Yahwists in Babylon.

Ezekiel's destiny appears here in a curious light. Previously his compatriots cherished the dangerous illusion that God would protect them in the final resort against the horror of national annihilation, but Ezekiel foretold terrible and very full punishment. Now that the Chosen People had experienced the very depths of misfortunes and believed that all was lost irreparably, the prophet began to preach a doctrine of dazzling hope. The God of the Covenant, he proclaimed, was almighty and present in all places – even there, on the banks of the Euphrates. Had not he, Ezekiel, seen with his own eyes the 'glory' of the Lord in that dazzling theophany in which the Assyro-Babylonian Karibu, guardians of the temples and servants of the pagan gods, were harnessed to the chariot of Yahweh? This strange and splendid vision was an affirmation of the true God's transcendence, and also of his omnipresence, which was no longer to be regarded as tied to the Holy of Holies in the Temple which was now destroyed.

The people were not to be discouraged. Yahweh was the Almighty. From dry bones he could cause a new people to rise (the vision of Ezekiel, 37:1–14).

Prediction of the return of the exiles to a Palestine renewed

Ezekiel solemnly foretold that, freed from the pagans (Ammonites and Edomites) who had settled there, the Promised Land would shortly see the return of the exiles. And there the People of God, made clean at last, would be united to Yahweh by a very close and universal Covenant.

This implied a complete reorganization of the community; the temptations and abuses which had led Israel to its ruin would have to be eliminated. And this was how the prophet saw the future of the Chosen People, reformed into one nation and re-established on Mount Zion.

It would be a perfect kingdom, equally divided among the tribes (Ezk. 48). For perfect worship there would be a perfect Temple whose carefully established and fully detailed plan Ezekiel had received. The plan could not be carried out, perhaps, topographically or architecturally, and must probably be regarded as a symbolic view of Judaism. Thus Yahweh would once more dwell in his Temple. From the sanctuary in Jerusalem would flow the celebrated spring of water (Ezk. 47:1–12) bringing fertility even to Arabah, the sterile plain to the south of the Dead Sea whose waters would then be sweetened. This was a symbol of the divine presence which would be manifested throughout the entire country and would be manifested throughout the entire country and would penetrate each faithful soul and there cause the seeds of holiness to germinate.

But the children of Israel were not yet to count on Yahweh's definitive victory. Gog, King of Magog, the figure of Anti-Christ and the Prince of Evil, would endeavour to overthrow the theocratic organization which would then have been established in Jerusalem. In the time to come Israel would once more experience many disappointments before seeing the manifestation of the fullness of divine glory in the Promised Land.

Prophecy of the Shepherd and Messiah (Ezk. 34)

This coming of the Shepherd, a symbol of the king, the ideal leader ardently desired by all, is nothing new in the Bible. Why was this shepherd so ardently desired?

Simply to take the place of the wicked shepherds of the flock whose blindness has disqualified them. Thus they are to be dismissed. It is God himself who will bestow on the body of his faithful followers one Shepherd, the 'Messiah', he who is called 'my Servant'.

Ezekiel's spiritual and doctrinal contribution

At the outset Ezekiel, as we have observed, appeared as one of the most active of workers for Judaism, with his impetuous desires for national renaissance and religious regeneration. He laid the foundations of a remodelling of worship which came to constitute the line of defence of Yahwism against the seductive attraction of paganism.

The great spiritual reform effected by Ezekiel consisted in the proclamation of a spiritual religion; it is with the heart that a man makes contact with his Creator.

Then at the more theological level we find him going further than the teaching of Israelite monotheism which was far too inclined to regard Yahweh as the national God, betaking himself at pleasure to the Temple in Jerusalem to deliver his oracles. The sanctuary had just been destroyed by the will of God himself as a punishment for his rebellious people. But Yahweh still continued his glorious and everlasting reign. Thus the prophet proclaimed that Yahweh was the God not only of the land of Canaan, but the God of the universe, the sovereign Master of the world.

II. The life of the Judaean exiles in Babylon, from the death of Nebuchadnezzar to the appearance of the liberator (altogether, about thirteen years, 562–549)

Nebuchadnezzar was too authoritarian a sovereign to allow any group of prisoners of war to hold up their heads. Those Judaeans who were incautious enough to venture on any move towards revolt were thrown into prison, sold as slaves or, more simply, put to death. Fortunately, Ezekiel's preaching, which was entirely religious in nature, was not regarded as subversive by the Babylonian authorities; the prophet had permission to speak freely. But no real changes in the treatment of the prisoners could be observed during the first fifteen years of the captivity.

The material life of the Judaeans on the banks of the Euphrates

Directly after Nebuchadnezzar's death (562), a considerable change can be seen in the living conditions of the exiles.

Avilmarduk, the new monarch of Babylon, eager to alleviate the lot of the unfortunate Jehoiachin, who had been a prisoner for thirty-seven years (2 Kings 24:27–30), allowed him to eat at the royal table. During the reign of this new sovereign and his short-lived successors the more humane nature of the government was manifested in the progressive slackening of control of the prisoners.

A number of exiled Judaeans started business as merchants and some of them even succeeded in making large fortunes. Some of them, who ten years previously had arrived in this foreign land as exiles, by this time possessed large estates and thousands of slaves (Ezk. 2:65).

The religious activity of the Judaeans in Babylon

On many occasions the faith of several of the Judaeans seems to have been rather wavering, but a 'small remnant' remembered having heard the voices of the prophets in the recent past. This nucleus of faithful Yahwists preserved in their hearts a tender memory of Yahweh's protection. Thus when the exiles began to be fairly free to organize themselves the first concern was to form a group around their spiritual leaders, who continually encouraged them and fostered the hope that they should place in their God and Protector. For this purpose they used to meet, first under Ezekiel and afterwards under certain 'elders' in some private houses; there the sacred books were read, they were reminded of the principal themes of the preaching of the prophets, the Law was explained; with care and spiritual profit they meditated on the word of God. Under the direction of a presiding elder or a scribe the sons of Abraham once more came together in community to receive religious teaching and to take part in prayer in common. This was the origin of the organized worship which, at a later date, at the time of the diaspora, was to become the synagogue.

The Judaeans continued to use their Hebrew language, although at this period Aramean was beginning to be used fairly generally in the Jewish colonies in Babylon. The colonies of exiles visited each other and corresponded: they wrote to their co-religionists in Jerusalem and remained in close touch with them. National unity was thus founded on a solid basis.

In this foreign land their leaders took good care that the people did not forget their ancestral traditions and religious anniversaries. With increased fervour, and so far as the new circumstances of their lives enabled them to do so, the exiles celebrated the great festivals: the Passover, Pentecost, the feast of Tabernacles, the day of Atonement *(Yom ha-Kippurim)* and many others besides. With a severity unknown in the happier days of life in Canaan they kept the laws about circumcision and the sabbath. They observed the law prohibiting unclean foods very carefully and also the fasts of devotion.

But it is the spiritualization of religion that should be emphasized here. Many of the faithful began to understand that submission to the will of God, obedience to the Law and prayer of the heart were certainly more efficacious than the sacrificial offering of animals in the Temple court. On this point the ancient as well as the more recent prophets had endeavoured to enlighten the followers of Yahweh. Two centuries previously Amos and Hosea had already cried out:

> 'I reject your oblations,
> and refuse to look at your sacrifices of fattened cattle . . .
> For it is love that I desire and not sacrifices; the knowledge of God and not burnt offerings.'

More recently Ezekiel had insisted on the outstanding value of interior prayer, prayer from the heart. A small group of Judaeans, torn by the sufferings of exile, began to understand the need for a spiritual transformation to bring them nearer to God.

There were, of course, a certain number of apostates who were led away by the great splendour of the Chaldaean ceremonies. But gathered round the spiritual leaders there was a faithful nucleus which maintained the flame of Yahwism in all its purity. They had come to understand the great truth that, on the day when they would be allowed to return to Jerusalem and rebuild the Temple there could be no question of returning to the former errors and disastrous compromises; the theocratic society, re-established on new foundations, would have to be inspired by genuine faith based on the Law of Yahweh.

The literary activity of the Judaean exiles in Babylon

The material heritage had disappeared with the fall of Jerusalem. Fortunately, they had been able to save what belonged to the historical and juridical heritage. In the two wheeled chariots, of the kind represented on the

Chaldaean bas-reliefs, had been hidden a great number of those scrolls on which scribes in Jerusalem and Samaria had copied the sacred texts. In addition to the carrying of these traditions of Israel to Babylon there must also be taken into account the prodigious oriental memory which could retain without difficulty chapter after chapter of the Law.

Very soon there occurred an amazing manifestation of literary activity in legal and historical matters among the exiled Judaeans.

The materials that the exiles had at their disposal quite certainly numbered hundreds of scrolls; but it was all complete disorder. There were obviously contradictory legislative texts of different periods. What had to be done, then, was to examine this great mass of legal material, and to eliminate from it all the ancient decisions which were no longer in accord with conditions then prevailing. The laws also had to be arranged as logically as possible in harmony with the needs of daily life. In addition, the whole body of material needed to be completed, to be connected together and classified to form a coherent body of law.

Work of a similar nature was required with the historical material. Some of the scrolls dealt with episodes of the period of the Judges: they related what had occurred in the northern Israelite region. Others dealing with the same subject were however concerned with events occurring in the southern Judaean kingdom. In addition, there was information of the greatest interest about the life of David, but there was nothing about Samuel. By chance, that was related elsewhere. One scroll set forth the history of the Judaean monarchy with no mention at all of the schismatic kings who occupied the throne of Samaria.

In short, there was no attempt at synthesis. The whole

mass of material was in a fragmentary state, without connection or order. It is to the honour of the literary group in Babylon that they managed to achieve a methodical classification and clarification of the texts by adding the required explanations to this mass of information.

The preparation of this admirable work was due exclusively to the scribes deported to Babylon. These learned jurists and historians produced a work that can really be termed monumental; it emerged as the legal and historical corpus; from these two elements they formed a single entity as complete as it was possible to be; this was the lively and authentic account of the adventure of Israel.

In the time of Hezekiah (716–687) there was a similar attempt at unification and in the reign of Josiah (640–609) a sort of academy had also begun to make a collection of national traditions. But there was nothing comparable, really, with the effort made and the result achieved by the scribes of the Exile. Here we have an immense deuteronomic fresco: the Book of Joshua, the Book of Judges, the Books of Samuel, the Books of Kings.

The authors of this great history of Israel remained anonymous.

It would be quite wrong to confuse these scribes with their predecessors – priests of the Temple or officials of the royal household, responsible for recopying, commenting and, if necessary, clarifying the texts of the ancient scrolls. It was a humble enough part that they played on occasion though that in no way excluded their being 'inspired' in accordance with Jewish traditions.

The men of learning who thus set to work in exile possessed a thorough knowledge of the Scriptures. They were men of God, their souls imbued with the

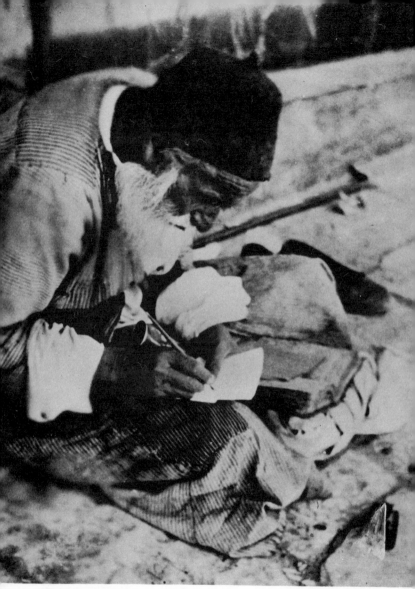

These are the words of the book written in Babylon by Baruch son of Neraiah, son of Mahseiah, son of Zedekiah, son of Hasadiah, in the fifth year, on the seventh day of the month, at the time when the Chaldaens captured Jerusalem and burned it down.

Baruch 1:1—2

teaching of the sacred books. In difficult cases their contemporaries came to consult them, just as nowadays people ask advice of a legal expert or a theologian. They then solved the difficulties, indicating the religious or legal solution to be adopted. In a short time they were given the title, which they certainly deserved, of 'doctors of the law'. This was an indication of the importance of their social or religious function, for in the civilization of Israel the two functions were usually indistinguishable. These doctors were held in equal reverence with the prophet and the priest. Indeed, after the Exile, when there were no more prophets, the 'doctors of the law' were of greater importance than the priestly class and were to become real guides of Israel.

The return to Judah an illusion?

The Mesopotamian authorities, whether Assyrian or Chaldaean, were the originators of the system of deporting the populations of rebel countries. Up to this time the conquerors had never allowed prisoners of war to return to their native country. With some show of reason the governments of these countries regarded these successive additions of foreign manpower as a vary valuable national asset, since usually the reported peoples were quickly integrated into the native population; and this was entirely to the state's advantage.

Yet all the prophets, from Isaiah to Ezekiel, proclaimed quite clearly that the terrible trial laid on Israel by Yahweh would be a heavy punishment certainly, but a temporary one. It was impossible to doubt the different revelations of the great prophets whose predictions were always fulfilled. The 'remnant', which in misfortune and by meditation had come to an understanding of Yahweh's plan, awaited with unshaken confidence the fulfilment of the promise — their early return to the Promised Land.

For the historian in modern times who examines the political scene of the Middle East at that period, there seems no likelihood of such a return occurring. Towards the end of the sixth century B.C. the Middle East had only recently been divided into three great kingdoms and at that time seemed quite stable.

Examination of the map shows that the Assyrian empire had been shared out between two conquerors, Babylon and Media. The king of Babylon took the valley of the Euphrates, as well as the vassal provinces of the west (Syria) and the south (Canaan) as far as the Egyptian frontier. The king of Media had settled in the valley of the Tigris, incorporating in his new dominions the provinces situated, roughly speaking, to the north of the river.

In addition, in Asia Minor, the State of Lydia had just been established, with Sardis as its capital, governed by the celebrated Croesus. His territory stretched from the west of Median Cappadocia and Babylonian Cilicia as far as the Aegean Sea.

These three sovereigns of Babylon, Media and Lydia seemed to have no ideas of supremacy; in any case they appeared to have no intention of engaging in a general conflict whose outcome would remain very uncertain.

It should be added, for the account to be complete, that Egypt, then extremely weak, refrained for the time being from causing trouble in the way that she had often done in the past.

It was a rare occurrence for the Middle East to be so quiet.

Just at this time among the Jewish communities of the Euphrates a group of exiles awaited in complete faith the appearance of an unknown conqueror. According to the prophecies he was to bring fire and the sword to the whole of the Fertile Crescent from the coasts of the

Persian Gulf to the land of the pharaohs. He would cut in pieces the armies which attempted to stand in the way of his triumphal progress, he would overthrow kings and enter all the capitals as a conqueror. Proud Babylon would have to bend the knee. Finally, in a gesture of generosity unprecedented in history, he would authorize the deported Jews to return to the land of their fathers. The 'remnant' would then be able to return to Jerusalem; they would even be allowed to rebuild the Temple of Yahweh destroyed by Nebuchadnezzar's rage.

Ideas of this kind might appear almost to be the product of a fevered imagination. And yet it was just in this way that events turned out.

III. Liberation of the remnant of Judah (549–538)
The great powers seemed to have no intention of going to war. It looked as if it might be a period of peace for the nations situated between Mesopotamia and the valley of the Nile. But the Middle East was always in a state of ferment, and the peace could not last for long.

Cyrus, a petty king of Media
At the time of the Assyrian empire we witnessed the arrival of the Indo-European hordes which were known to the Assyrians as Medes, Scythians or Persians. The Assyrians were eager to incorporate them in their armies as mercenaries.

These waves of invaders came from southern Asia, from a region to the south of the Pamir tableland where the nucleus of the Aryan group had just originated. Some of them made for India where they became the Aryans. Other branches turned towards Europe where their tribes settled in territories to which they gave their name – Gaul, Germany, Doria, Anglia, Italy etc. Those with whom we are here concerned went to the region that is now called the Middle East. These newcomers to the Semitic world took advantage of the decay of the Assyrian empire (606) to settle in the mountainous region of Iran (Persia) and in the valleys of Susiana.

Like all primitive Aryan societies they possessed a military organization of feudal type. At the period now concerning us — that is, the middle of the sixth century B.C. — in the neighbourhood of Susa there was living a petty local chieftain with a few tribes of Medes under his rule; proudly he bore the title of king of Anshan. His name was Cyrus. He owed allegiance to Astyages, the powerful king of the confederation known under the general name of the Medes.

Cyrus was ambitious; he knew his own worth; he was eager to demonstrate his military genius on the battle-field. In 555 he decided that the time for action had come.

Thrones topple

There followed a series of brilliant victories.

555: First of all Cyrus attacked his own sovereign, Astyages, son of Cyaxares. At first the struggle was hard. From Media the campaign moved into Persian territory. Pasargades, the provincial capital, was finally captured by Cyrus. Astyages was taken prisoner. It was now the turn of Ecbatana, the capital of Media; Cyrus seized the city with its enormous riches; these he had taken to Anshan.

It should be noted that the victor — an Aryan whose traditions differed from those of the Semitic east — spared the life of his royal prisoner. Indeed, he took pleasure in surrounding him with a certain respect. Nor did he burn the cities which fell into his hands or massacre their inhabitants. This was a considerable change from methods initiated a few centuries previously by the Assyrians and followed by the Chaldaeans.

194

After this first series of victories Cyrus took the high sounding title of 'king of the Medes and Persians' (549).

All this occurred on the very threshold of Babylon. The Judaeans in exile began to look towards the young conqueror who might well be called to upset the established political system.

Croesus, king of Lydia, reigned over Asia Minor. In his capital city of Sardis he heard of the fall of Astyages, his brother-in-law. At once Croesus organized a formidable coalition comprising Nabonides, king of Babylon, Amasis of Egypt and Sparta, whose troops were already renowned in Asia for their high standard of training.

Croesus thought that he was strong enough to attack his opponent before the arrival of his allies. It was a mistake. After a number of indecisive battles he was obliged to retreat to Sardis, where he shut himself up. Before the allies could arrive to help him Cyrus had taken the city by storm (546).

After the surrender of the king of Lydia, Cyrus' empire extended from Persia to the Aegean Sea by way of the valley of the Tigris, that is, all that was formerly Assyria. To make himself master of the whole of this part of Asia Cyrus had now only Babylon to deal with. It was considerably weakened by reason of the lack of energy of its king. Nabonides, who was almost weak-minded. He was indifferent to the business of his office and spent all his time on the restoration of ancient Mesopotamian cults.

At any moment the invincible Persian armies were expected in the valley of the Euphrates. And the small colonies of exiled Israelites feverishly awaited with undisguised joy the arrival of the formidable king who would allow them, they had not a doubt, to return to Jerusalem.

Deutero-Isaiah, or the second Isaiah (546–539)

It is in this expectant atmosphere that must be placed the prophet known, for want of a better name, as the second Isaiah or Deutero-Isaiah.[5]

In a lyrical, and sometimes explosive style this messenger of the 'good news' foretells for the unfortunate Judaeans, his companions in exile, the imminent arrival of Cyrus, the providential saviour raised up by Yahweh to overthrow the Babylonian dynasty. Cyrus is described as the liberator of Israel and on this occasion the prophet bestows on the king of the Persians the most high-sounding titles:

> *'Thus says Yahweh to his anointed, to Cyrus*
> *whom he has taken by his right hand*
> *to subdue nations before him.'*　　(Is. 45:1)

After the victory of the great conqueror over the Chaldaean princes, Israel will set off through the wilderness, over the route leading from Babylon to the Promised Land. To complete his work, Cyrus — it is Yahweh speaking —

> *will rebuild my city* [Jerusalem],
> *will bring my exiles back.*　　(Is. 45:13)

Hopefully the Judaeans awaited the deliverance which, they felt, could not now be long delayed.

Seven years of waiting

Cyrus was right on the threshold of Babylonia when, to the anguished amazement of the Jews of Nippur, he

[5] Second Isaiah: he is thus called because the collection of his prophecies has been placed directly after those of Isaiah (Isaiah, *Book of the Consolation of Israel,* chapters 40–55). For a long time biblical scholars hesitated to separate these two parts which, nevertheless, are dissimilar in style and historical setting. The latter indeed is two centuries later than the descriptions given by Isaiah in the seventh century. Today, most Catholic exegetes admit that the chapters of the Book of Isaiah 40–55, are the masterly work of a contemporary of Cyrus, that is, of a prophet of the school of Isaiah living during the last years of the Exile.

turned away from the valley of the Euphrates towards the east. Tactically his plan can be easily explained; he wished to protect recent and future contests against the assaults of the formidable Aryan migrations from the Asian hinterland. He himself was an Indo-European and he was well aware of the military qualities and the insatiable territorial appetites of these people. Warlike peoples had just settled beyond Iran and they were preparing to migrate next towards the Mediterranean countries. It was urgent to bring them to heel at once. And so we find Cyrus penetrating as far as Afghanistan; he pushed on then towards the barbarous regions of Sogdiana, finally fixing the frontier of his empire on the river Jaxartes (today the Syr Daria) to the south of the Aral Sea. It was an immense empire stretching from the shores of the Aegean sea, opposite Greece, to the north of India.

Clearly these campaigns required long and sustained effort, and hard fighting. The years went by. In Babylon the Jewish exiles, losing hope, were very worried. They wondered whether Cyrus would ever return in the direction of Mesopotamia. And there was the danger, they felt, that he might be killed in some far off battle. All their dreams of the restoration of Israel seemed doomed to failure.

The Second Isaiah did his best to revive their hopes; continually he foretold the coming return of Cyrus and the destruction of Babylon. But the time of waiting was long and they began to despair.

The Second Isaiah: prophet of deliverance

The Second Isaiah should not be regarded merely as a prophet whose only function was to foretell historical events which were soon to occur.

In a book like the present, which is intended to remain

strictly historical there could be no question of giving a detailed analysis of the dynamic new teaching of this prophet. It should however be observed, firstly, that Deutero-Isaiah was the first to have proclaimed monotheism in no uncertain voice. This fundamental notion, had, of course, been expressed by most of the prophets from Elijah to Ezekiel. But with the Second Isaiah we see monotheism assuming the definitive form which is the distinctive feature of the religion of Israel. Henceforward, Yahweh is the only God, the universal God, the everlasting God. *'I am the first and the last. Save for me, there are no gods. I am God; from all eternity, I am God.'*

The second message from Deutero-Isaiah dealt with the problem of the suffering which falls on the righteous.

Hitherto there had been no idea of a reward after life; God rewarded man here below; those who observed the commandments would have blessings heaped on them while the wicked would be overwhelmed with misfortunes. Now it is enough to look at the world around us to know that things are very far from always turning out like that. An attempt had been made to explain these cases by the fact that children often pay for the sins of their parents. We have seen that Jeremiah and then Ezekiel spoke against these ideas; according to the prophets everyone will be judged according to their personal merits. But this hardly throws any light on the question; the sufferings of the righteous remain incomprehensible.

The Second Isaiah provides the theological key to the problem: the suffering of the righteous man brings the whole community closer to God. It brings about the redemption of the sinful community.

Isaiah had begun to understand the lofty role that had fallen on the 'remnant', on the tiny Judaean nucleus deported to the 'water of Babylon'. The prophet had grasped the real meaning of the frightful moral trials experienced by the exiles; it was a question of expiating, of wiping out the sins of Israel. Here we have a concept that was to occupy a pre-eminent place in Christian theology.

Finally, the prophet depicts for us the figure of him whom he calls the 'Servant' — a righteous man smitten by the Creator, disfigured by suffering and put to a shameful death.

He was pierced through for our faults,
crushed for our sins.
On him lies a punishment that brings us peace,
and through his wounds we are healed . . .

Harshly dealt with he bore it humbly,
he never opened his mouth,
like a lamb that is led to the slaughter house,
like a sheep that is dumb before its shearers
never opening its mouth . . .

Yes, he was torn away from the land of the living;
for our faults struck down in death.
(Is. 53:5, 7, 8)

Thus the suffering 'Servant' is a mysterious personage who represents all his people. He is probably a prophet who is to come, a Wise man, perhaps a Saviour.

He is the Messiah.

An entirely new idea takes its place in human thought. The realization grows that an animal victim, unconscious of its role when it is offered on the sacrificial stone, could be replaced by another victim, a human victim, who would offer himself willingly for the salvation of his executioners.

We reach here the very heights of prophetic revelation.

Cyrus marches on Babylon

Cyrus had just finished establishing the defensive barrier that he required at the eastern borders of his empire. His hands were now free. He determined to march on Babylon.

For this greater soldier an expedition of this kind would have seemed like a mere military excursion. Nabonides, king of Babylon, was an odd figure whose principal concern was to make a collection of the statues of the principal deities of the valley of the Euphrates. This, it seemed to him, would amply suffice for the defence of his kingdom. Moreover, he had left almost all the government to his son, Belshazzar, a weak and incapable creature.

Although he was a long way from Babylon, Cyrus had made careful preparations in the country; paid agitators continually criticized the government, while proclaiming the imminent arrival of this ideal and humane king of Persia who would inaugurate a period of happiness.

In the region of Nippur the Judaeans were by no means the last to acclaim this news. They already saw themselves on the road to Jerusalem.

In 540 B.C. Cyrus appeared in Babylonia. There is no information extant on the first part of this campaign.

Then, Gabaru, one of Cyrus' best generals, advanced down the lower valley of the Tigris, and at Opis cut the Chaldaean forces in pieces; the road to Babylon was open.

Nabonides advanced to Sippar, a stronghold a short distance to the north of the capital; a Persian army swamped it and put it shamefully to flight (17th day of the month of *Tishri*, 539).

In Babylon, Belshazzar acted on the assumption that the fortifications of the city were impregnable; he made a show of spending his time in feasting. Many years later one of these banquets was made the setting for the Book of Daniel. Belshazzar saw on the wall opposite him *the fingers of a human hand* which *began to write on the plaster of the palace wall* the words *Mene, Mene, Tekel* and *Parsin*. Daniel explained the hidden meaning of these words to the king (Daniel 5).[6]

Two days after capturing Sippar the invading army, still under Gabaru's command, laid siege to Babylon (16th day of the month *Tishri*, September–October 539). The capital fell after being besieged for a fortnight. Herodotus informs us that the Persians entered the city by surprise, after diverting the course of the Euphrates. There are many difficulties about this theory and modern scholars think rather that a fifth column in Cyrus' pay merely opened the gates of the city to the besiegers. In any case, the palaces, temples and private houses were strictly respected; the population did not suffer any violence. In pursuance of his policy Cyrus was determined to appear as a liberator; he proclaimed safety and welfare for the whole of Babylon.

Cyrus, king of Babylon; inauguration of a humane and tolerant policy

In the time of the Assyrians and Babylonians the Mesopotamian States appeared as predatory nations; war had become a national industry, and a profitable one. It was a matter not only of seizing vast territories but also of systematically emptying the annexed countries of their wealth and populations for the benefit of the conqueror.

---

[6] *Mene:* 'God has *measured* the Chaldaean kingdom.' *Tekel:* 'He has *weighed* the monarch and his weight has been found wanting.' *Parsin:* 'Babylon will be divided and its territory given to Cyrus, king of the *Persians*.'

The behaviour of Cyrus, who belonged to the Indo-European race, was very different from these Semitic methods. This Aryan, a fire-worshipper, was a follower of the ancient Asiatic dualist religion, according to which Ormazd, the god of good, was in conflict with the god of evil, Ahriman. The faithful adherent of this religion was the liegeman of Ormazd and he had to struggle within himself against Ahriman, the dark personage who continually incited him to do sinful actions. There were no temples and no images, but a lofty morality whose severe regulations can be discerned in the texts of the Avesta.[7]

After the fall of Babylon, Cyrus determined to establish a stable state in which the different peoples of his empire would be able to organize their lives in peace.

The Judaeans made no secret of their disappointment at Cyrus's behaviour in not massacring the Babylonians and burning down the city, for the prophets had foretold the exemplary punishment of this hated city. The prophecies of the misfortunes of Babylon were not to be fulfilled until much later, actually in 485 when Xerxes meted out severe punishment for a rebellion of the Babylonians. Israel's hatred was no affair of Cyrus'. He was eager to preserve the whole of this fine city, the most beautiful in the world.

This action was in strict accordance with his political ideals. He endeavoured to bind his peoples to him by the benefits that he conferred on them.

Cyrus gives all the exiles in Babylon their freedom and their gods

One of Cyrus's first actions was to allow the numerous

[7] In actual fact we only know primitive Iranian religion through the sacred books of a date later than the times of Cyrus; these were drawn up a century after the events studied here. These texts appear to be the work of the celebrated reformer Zarathustra.

colonies of exiles settled in the valley of the Euphrates to return, if they so wanted, to their country of origin. He tried in this way to pacify these peoples; it was in the interests of the central government to get rid of those little pockets of resistance which, in the very nature of things, subsisted among the exiles. The joy of these displaced people, so providentially set free, may well be imagined. Soon, throughout the empire, a concert of praise could be heard in honour of the merciful king.

Very cunningly, Cyrus venerated the gods of the nations made vassals by his predecessors. In Babylon he solemnly proclaimed that Marduk, the god of the Chaldaean capital, had called him personally to occupy the throne of Nabonides. In addition Cyrus showed such deep respect to Yahweh that the Judaeans actually imagined for a time that he was ready to acknowledge the God of Israel as the only true God; they even thought that he was going to work for the establishment of the reign of Yahweh of Jerusalem over the territory of the empire.

The Chaldaeans not only deported the population of conquered countries; they also took away the idols of their temples and set them up in Babylon. Cyrus ordered the return of the statues of these gods (which in their turn had become prisoners of war) and all the ritual objects confiscated by Nebuchadnezzar and his successors. It is difficult to know which to admire more: Cyrus' political shrewdness or his amazing liberalism.

Cyrus' decree concerning the Judaeans of Babylon

The exiles from Jerusalem, of course, were included in this measure. The Bible gives two versions of the decree of Cyrus concerning the freeing of the exiles from Jerusalem. The first (Ezr. 1:1–14) could well be a version of the proclamation made in Hebrew to the exiles. The second version (headed Memorandum) was probably written down for the Persian archivists; it may be regarded as a summary of the original (Ezr. 6:1–5).

The Book of Ezra tells how the document was discovered. At the time of King Darius of Persia *a search was made in Babylonia in the muniment rooms where the archives were kept;* at Ecbatana[8] a scroll containing the famous edict was found. It ran as follows:

Memorandum

In the first year of Cyrus the king,[9] King Cyrus decreed:

Temple of God in Jerusalem

The Temple will be rebuilt as a place at which sacrifices are to be offered and to which offerings are brought to be burnt. Its height is to be sixty cubits, its width sixty cubits.[10] There are to be three thicknesses of stone blocks and one of wood.[11] The expense is to be met by the king's household.[12] Furthermore, the vessels of gold and silver from the Temple of God[13] which Nebuchadnezzar took from the sanctuary in Jerusalem and brought to Babylon are to be restored so that everything may be restored to the sanctuary and put back in the Temple of God.[14]

(Ezr. 6:3–5)

[8] Ecbatana in the mountains of Media; the scroll was found in the palace where the Persian kings spent the summer months. This would seem to indicate that Cyrus must have published his edict during the summer which followed the capture of Babylon (538).

[9] First years of his reign as king of Babylon, that is, in 538.

[10] These measurements do not agree with those of the first Temple (see in this series, *Solomon,* page 78). Here the text is possibly corrupt (see *Jerusalem Bible,* note *b* to Ezr. 6:3).

[11] Wood: the reference is to the panelling lining the three rooms of the Temple.

[12] That is, by the central government of Babylon. It is very probable that a part of the taxes raised in Judah, instead of being sent to Babylon were allotted to the building of the Temple in Jerusalem.

[13] A list of them is extant: golden offering cups, 30; silver offering cups, 1,029; golden cups, 30; silver cups, 410; other vessels, 1,000.

[14] There is no mention of the Ark of the Covenant, nor of the cherubim. We can guess the fate of the latter; they must have been broken up and stripped of the gold plate which covered them. It must be supposed that the Ark of the Covenant and the Tables of the Law which it contained during the last days of the siege of Jerusalem were hidden by the priests, the guardians of the Temple. They must certainly have placed the Ark, with the Tables of the Law inside it in a very secret

It is a mistake to attempt to explain the edict of Cyrus, as does Josephus the Jewish historian, by supposing that the new king of Babylon was acquainted with the prophecies of Deutero-Isaiah. The measure formed part, as we have shown, of a general one which referred to all the exiled population.

Preparation for the great return (538)

On the publication of Cyrus' edict itense excitement seized the Jewish communities of the Nippur region. The sons of the exiles who half a century previously had left Jerusalem in tears, and possibly even some of the survivors of the tragedy of 587, were at last able to return. Already they were talking of rebuilding the Temple with the financial help, of course, of the Babylonian authorities. And devout Yahwists, remembering the fulfilment of the many prophecies in the course of past centuries, gave continual thanks to Yahweh. Glorious days were beginning for the people of God.

Yet it must not be supposed that the enthusiasm was general. An appreciable proportion of the Judaeans had been led astray by the magnificent ceremonies which took place in the Babylonian temples. More numerous still were those who continued to practise idolatrous rites: fetishism, worship of the Baals 'under the green trees', sacrifices of the new-born, sacred prostitution and so on.

All these must be regarded as lost for Israel permanently. They would not return to Jerusalem.

There was the further category of those who, in spite of their faith, were loath to leave this rich country where,

---

place. (This was the Ark made at the foot of Sinai to Moses' orders.) It was not discovered in the following centuries. According to a Jewish tradition the Ark was carried to Mount Nebo where all trace of it is lost. This legend inspired 2 Mac. 1–9.

socially at least, they had been successful. After deportation they had eventually become wealthy landed
proprietors and the owners of many slaves; with real
distress they wondered whether they would return to
the same position of importance and the same prosperity
in Judah with its unprofitable soil. Shrewd men of
business, they had contrived to make real fortunes as
merchants whose commercial interests extended far
beyond Mesopotamia. In addition there were the
Israelites who occupied important posts at the Babylonian court, especially in the financial department.

Of course, they shared the feelings of those who were
making ready for their departure; but they had not the
courage to leave behind their comfort, their well-ordered
lives, their wealth. They confined their activity to sending
subsidies to their former companions in captivity who in
Judah, in the ruins of the Temple, were putting up the
walls of the sanctuary and rebuilding the Temple of
Yahweh. These capitalists felt unable to follow the
caravan which was preparing to return to the city of
David.

The whole expedition was organized with amazing
rapidity. Lists were drawn up, the people were assembled
according to their villages of origin in Judah, and leaders
were chosen; the departure dates were settled so that
parties would leave at fixed intervals.

The Babylonian captivity had come to an end. The
Chosen People organized their return home as they sang
the praises of Yahweh.

The 'Remnant' of Israel

In the next volume, dealing with the *Rebirth of Israel*,
the preparations for departure and the events of the
journey are described. On its long road home we shall
follow the 'remnant' of Israel, the tiny minority which,

despite the dark tragedies that it had experienced, or rather because of them, had managed to preserve consciousness of its lofty mission.

There is no comparison here with the wretched band of Judaean prisoners who, fifty years previously, had been snatched from their burning city. The men who were now marching towards Jerusalem had emerged from the crucible of suffering purified, transformed, and ready now to work effectively, and with full knowledge of what they were doing, for the 'Rebirth of Israel'.

In the whole adventure of the People of God, the Exile is the key to their history. No other social or religious group could have withstood such an experience. Not merely did Israel survive its terrible trial, but it emerged from it stronger, more unconquerable and more resolute than ever.

Ezekiel's prophecy was beginning to come true:

'I am going to take you from among the nations and gather you together from all the foreign countries, and bring you home to your own land. I shall pour clean water over you and you will be cleansed; I shall cleanse you of all your defilement and all your idols. I shall give you a new heart and put a new spirit in you; I shall remove the heart of stone from your bodies and give you a heart of flesh instead. I shall put my spirit in you, and make you keep my laws and sincerely respect my observances. You will live in the land which I gave your ancestors. You shall be my people and I will be your God' (Ezk. 36:24–28).

SELECT BIBLIOGRAPHY

The Jerusalem Bible; Darton, Longman & Todd (London).
Doubleday and Co. Inc. (N.Y.).

General Books

The Jerome Bible Commentary; Chapman (London)
A Catholic Commentary on Holy Scripture; Nelson
(London)
Peake's Commentary on the Bible; Nelson (London)
Atlas of the Bible; L. H. Grollenberg, O.P.; Nelson
(London)
J. Bright: *A History of Israel;* S.C.M. Press (London),
Westminster Press (Philadelphia)
C. Charlier: *The Christian Approach to the Bible;* Sands
Publishers (Glasgow)
L. Johnston: *A History of Israel;* Sheed and Ward
(London and New York)
T. Maertens, O.S.B.: *Bible Themes;* Darton, Longman &
Todd (London), Fides Publishers Inc. (Indiana)
J. L. McKenzie, S.J.: *Dictionary of the Bible;* Chapman
(London), The Bruce Publishing Company (Mil-
waukee)
R. de Vaux, O.P.: *Ancient Israel;* Darton, Longman &
Todd (London), McGraw-Hill Book Company (New
York)

Books about the Kingdom, the Prophets and the Exile

P. Ackroyd: *The Exile and the Restoration;* S.C.M. (London)

E. W. Heaton: *The Old Testament Prophets;* Penguin Books (London)

A. J. Heschel: *The Prophets;* . . . . . (New York)

G. Knight: *Prophets of Israel, (1), Isaiah;* Bible Guides, Abingdon Press (. . . . .)

J. Lindblom: *Prophecy in Ancient Israel;* Muhlenberg Press (Philadelphia), Oxford University Press

H. G. May: *Ezekiel;* Interpreters' Bible; . . . . . (New York)

C. R. North: *Isaiah 40–55;* Torch Bible Commentaries, S.C.M. Press (London)

J. Rhymer: *The Prophets and the Law;* Sheed & Ward (London), Pflaum Press (Ohio)

H. H. Rowley: *Men of God: Studies in Old Testament History and Prophecy;* Nelson (London)

N. H. Snaith: *The Book of Amos;* . . . . . (London)

B. Vawter: *The Conscience of Israel;* Sheed & Ward (London & New York)

J. M. Ward: *Hosea: A Theological Commentary;* . . . . . (New York)

A. C. Welch: *Jeremiah, His Time and His Work;* Oxford University Press

R. E. Wolfe: *Meet Amos and Hosea;* . . . . . (New York)

209

INDEX

Index

Nihil obstat: Lionel Swain, S.T.L., L.S.S.
Imprimatur: Victor Guazzelli, V.G.
Westminster, 23rd January 1970

DATE DUE